COWNOMICS

The *Holy* Cow—Fulcrum of a Civilization

By

ARTI AGARWAL

To request copyrights, please contact author at arti@cownomics.com

ISBN: 9781034662587

Cover design by: Arti Agarwal

Made in India

Contents

This book is dedicated to my ginger cat Cookie

Author's Note

I never thought of myself as a researcher, far less an author of a research-based book. But to light a flame doesn't require a forest fire. One stray spark is enough. It is enough to give enough light to brighten up a room, to consume the object it is burning. When the concept of saving cows (and other animals) as a much better way for an economy to function landed on me, I started working on it to the exclusion of almost everything else. It was not just an idea for me. It was a mission, one which I am working on even today.

Needless to say, I have had more than my fair share of failures on the way, some of which almost broke me mentally & emotionally, but there was something inside which insisted, persisted to keep burning on, whatever be the cost, whatever be the end. It was beyond me to back off. Those who know me will know that I have weathered severe problems with health, finances, work stress and many other things which have no name, but that is not some sort of a sacrifice. I am not interested in being some sort of a martyr or victim. I don't believe in those things. That is not something I see as my contribution. That is just indicative of the *size of the problem* we are trying to solve here. It takes something else to work on something like this, which goes against almost every "popular" and accepted narrative, or is so severely politicized, in almost every country in the world, that it becomes difficult to just have people listen to you, even if you are on the same side. Short term profits rule the world. Long held beliefs, habits, decadent systems, ideologies, biases all are part of the problem.

Writing this book has been a continuous tumbling-down-the-rabbit-hole of discoveries. I can say with certainty, that if the present me were to look back on the me of three years ago, I would look at that person and think her a fool—because I knew so little at that time. But I would also feel proud of the me of three years ago for having the right instincts and intuition to be willing to tumble down the rabbit hole. After all, before tumbling down, you have no idea what you are going to find, or how pleasant or easy it is going to be. It is diving blindsided. You don't know where you are going. But my instincts were right, and I am glad I did take the dive, because although taking that dive meant turning my whole life around, what I got out of it is worth it. I myself did not know the immense potential of what I am doing three years ago. I know now. And I want others to know it too.

I do not wish to continue in ciphers (although I do like cryptography). Saving the cow can save you, your economy and the planet. It is that simple. Ancient Hindus knew this, and their reverence for the cow was for this reason. They knew that the key to a healthy, wholesome, sustainable economy was possible only by nurturing the cow and other animals. Fast forward to now, the world is crashing around our ears, and if we do not fix our cruelty-based lifestyles soon, the effects of it will soon be in our faces, quite literally. They already are, actually, a plain as the nose on our faces, as the proverb goes, but we have chosen to not connect the dots and not heed all the warnings. When you ignore a few warnings, you get bigger warnings, and when you ignore that, comes the crash. I do not like the idea of a crash.

Unlike propagandist literature, I am not going to put a time scale to "how long we have." I don't know the depths of cruelty human beings are capable of achieving, so I cannot predict the time scale. But I do know one thing: when it comes to doing something good, something right, better now than later, better late then never.

Our current lifestyles which are exploitative, cruel, and insensitive to all that moves, impervious to the reasoning which tries to show how that is self-destructive, need to change. This book explains why and how. If you like it, do something about it. A good book review is nice, yes (thank you so much), but an actual tangible change in your own life is what will make this book work for you, for your country, for your—our—planet. If you hate the book, no problem. I am still glad you gave me a chance and decided to hear me out at least once. I thank you for that.

I only ask one thing of the reader—you—when you read this book, try not to see it through the lens of existing biases, political narratives, statements of influencers and celebrities, and a lot of the cacophony prevalent around these topics. Had I been satisfied with what people are saying and doing in these areas, I would have lived my life peacefully, never bothered with the book, and you would probably not even know who I am (which is perfectly fine, by the way). I decided to write this book because all the stories, opinions, theories around this subject are just floating around like free radicals, without any connections with each other, without any sense of purpose, without any forest to the trees. I have spent time building the proverbial forest, connecting the proverbial dots, and bringing a few age-old truths home. So, I beg of you, to read this book as if this is your first introduction to the subject. Just empty your cup before you fill it.

I have tried to keep this book short, so I don't kill you with boredom. But I will keep elaborating on this subject on my website cownomics.com, which will be updated with new research and findings, and hopefully my own experiments. So, if the book does intrigue you in the end, head over to the website for more. And with that, I think I have said everything I had to say about the book.

Arti Agarwal

8 March, 2021

Travesty of Travesties

The biggest travesty against humanity is making a sizable chunk of humanity believe that something that is going to destroy them is actually worth doing, and that something that can heal them is worthless. This reversal of beliefs, this indoctrination, so to say, is one of the biggest crimes against humanity. No international court or international organization may say so, but this, in reality, is how any civilization starts its march towards its complete destruction.

Cownomics (this book), is a step towards undoing one such travesty: the desecration of the place of the cow in the society, and the severe damage it is doing to entire humanity. Especially in Bharat, the land of *Rishis* (seers), *Munis* (sages), incarnations, and enlightened masters, the history of which is more than 20,000 years old, the cow was once a living deity worshiped by all. But today, she walks on roads, eating garbage, and is slaughtered whenever it becomes too "inconvenient" for her owner and the country folks to just feed her and give her shelter. This is not the failure of the cow, this is the failure of the ecosystem, which has failed to protect, nurture and worship the cow. This is a travesty which is hurting human beings in every possible way. In spite of access to the most sublime knowledge and science which can help people heal, grow, and evolve, people are currently choosing their own self destruction by creating and supporting a societal system which has no place for the cow.

"Cownomics," as you probably understand it today, before reading this book, is like a badly told story. It has lost links to the scientific research pointing to the impending disaster if the place of the cow is not restored. It has failed to get rooted in the original Vedic science that gives long term solutions for every aspect of the human existence. It is nothing more than a buzzword to abuse the divine principles shared with humanity by incarnations for their benefit. It is a hashtag used to fan political controversies, rather than a ground reality which sustains an entire ecosystem designed for health, prosperity, abundance, growth and well-being.

The purpose of this book is to set the meaning right, and show why true Cownomics is not just necessary, but rather, without it, you are speeding towards your inevitable, painful, sad END.

Meat eating is the outcome of a mindset that believes that it is perfectly "okay" to hurt or destroy others to get what you want. It is the outcome of a self-centered approach to life, which is blind to the suffering caused to others by one's action. But then it went one step further, and started hurting human beings and their own habitat, but because the link between the two was invisible, human beings did not even realize that they are hurting their own selves too, not just other creatures.

Cow as a Sentient, Sacred Being

Before we understand the scientific, economic and societal aspects of the cow, it is necessary to know the real place of the cow in the Hindu ecosystem. The Hindu view of the cow is not a mere ideology, but the reason why the cow was, and still is, ***the fulcrum of the Ganga Saraswati Civilization.*** That many people, including Hindus, today are unaware of it is a sad reality. But that ignorance does not alter the place originally given to the cow in the Hindu realms.

The core Hindu tenet is that everything is consciousness; everything is divine, vibrant, alive. Only the intensity and frequency of the extent to which consciousness reflects in an object varies, but everything is vibrating with the same cosmic consciousness. Consciousness is all pervading. The intensity of consciousness increases from single-cell organisms to multi-cell organisms, to plants to insects and other creatures, to animals, with human beings the most evolved species. Human beings are considered the most evolved species because the capacity to realize themselves as consciousness, and hence realize enlightenment, exists only in human beings. Other beings can grow and move further along this journey during the course of their lives. At the same time, everything that exists is a manifestation of that same divinity which we worship as *Ishwara*. We are not only all connected at our core, but in fact, there was never any disconnect between the billions of beings to begin with. **We always were, and always will be different, myriad manifestations of the same divinity, same cosmic consciousness.**

'Everything that exists is you'—this is the principle underlined in the Upanishads, Hindu scriptural texts.

In a famous quote, the enlightened Master Ramana Maharshi answered a seeker thus:

The seeker asked, "*Bhagwan*, how should we treat others?"

Maharshi answered, "*There are no others.*"

This is the essence of the Hindu philosophy vis-à-vis treatment of not just other people, but other beings, including animals. Whatever we do to others, we are actually meting out to our own selves. *Ahimsa*, or non-violence, is not just a moralistic principle in Hinduism, but meant to be a lifestyle, which is directly related to Hindu ideas of life, birth and death and non-duality of beings.

But was the cow really sacred?

India has been topping the charts in exports of beef. Naturally, the world over people are compelled to ask, "Is the cow really even sacred to Hindus?" It seems unfathomable that a people who pride themselves in worship of the cow could possibly by exporting tonnes of its slaughtered meat. Paradox as it may seem, it is true. **There are no paradoxes. We are just missing what might be hiding in plain sight.**

Cow is sacred to all sects and sub sects of Hinduism. From one *sampradaya* to another, one mutt to another, one temple to another, differences in practices, methods of worship, objects of worship and places of worship vary as infinitely as possible. Yet, two factors remain as unifiers of different sects of Hinduism - one being the sacred *pranava* sound *Om*, and the second, the cow.

This is because the cow has been sacred to Hindus since the very inception of the Vedic civilization. The source of all sects of Hinduism and Sanatana Dharma is the Vedas, Agamas and Upanishads—the source books of Hinduism, which give knowledge and understanding of cosmic truths (*jnana*) and what lifestyle (*charya*) a person should have, so as to be able to make these truths a part of their life, continuously evolving towards *Jeevan Mukti* (liberation while living) and *Moksha* (liberation at the time of death). These scriptures, which are "*Shruti*" text, are direct instructions of our deities like Shiva, Vishnu and their incarnations, recorded by Vedic *Rishis* (seers).

The cow was at the centre of the universe of the people of the Vedic civilization—the Ganga-Sarasvati civilization—which is thousands of years old. The cow finds innumerable mentions in the oldest of the Hindu scriptures—Vedas and Agamas. As mentioned in the Vedas, having many cows was a blessing. When the *yajmans* performing *yajnas* (fire rituals) asked for the *devatas* (deities) to be pleased and bless them, they asked them to endow them with numerous cows, calves and bulls. They asked the *devatas* like Indra and Agni to always protect their cows. They promise to look after the cows and pray to the cows to multiply in number quickly.

The cow was an established symbol of wealth and prosperity in the Vedic society.

In certain *yajnas*, the *yajmans* offer the *soma rasa* (elixir of immortality) to Devendra or Indra, and further add that the *soma rasa* has been mixed with the milk of cows, which has the same divine qualities as the *soma rasa* itself – thus making the *soma rasa* even more desirable and pleasing to Devaraj Indra.

It is mentioned that the divine rainwater which Devraj Indra showers on humans, is present in the milk of the cows as well.

चक्रं यदस्याप्स्वा निषत्तमुतो तदस्मै मध्विच्चच्छद्यात्

पृथिव्यामतिषितं यद्दूधः पयो गोष्वदधा ओषधीषु ।

Sam Veda, Chapter 10, Verse 9

"O yajmans! Indra is omnipresent in the Cosmos. He showers human beings with divine sweet water with his Vajra. The same water is present in the milk of cows and the juice of herbs, available to us."

It is also mentioned that the *soma rasa* exists in cows secretly.

ऋषिर्विप्रः पुर एता जनानामृभुर्धीर उशना काव्येन

स चिद्विवेद निहितं यदासामपीच्यां ३ गुह्यं नाम गोनाम् |

Samveda, Uttararchik, Chapter 1, Part 3, Verse 8

"Ushna Rishi is intelligent, knowledgeable, high achiever in Vedik sciences, patient, effulgent and a leader. The same Ushna Rishi, by means of stotras (songs of praise of devatas), received the Som Rasa secretly present in cows by great penance."

So, it is clearly stated that cows have the *soma rasa*, or the elixir of immortality. In several places, the *yajmans* refer to the items like milk obtained from the cow as a way to please the *devatas* and absolve themselves of their bad *karma*.

Thus, not the cow alone, but even all items obtained from the cow were considered sacred, and a way to achieve health, strength and ultimately, liberation.

The cow is mentioned as the epitome of motherliness, nurturing and wrapping herself around her calf, to protect it, and understands the unsaid words of the calf. She, thus, exceeds the intelligence of humans. Humans attempt to emulate these qualities of the cow.

गौरमीमेदनु वत्सं मिषन्तं मूर्धानं हिङ्ङकृणोन्मातवा ३

सृक्वाणं धर्ममभि वावशाना मिमाति मायुं पयते पयोभिः |

अयं स शिङ्क्ते येन गौरभीवृता मिमाति मायुं ध्वसनावधि श्रिता

सा चितिभिर्नि हि चकार मर्त्यं विद्युद्भवन्ती प्रति वव्रिमौहत ||

Rig Veda, Sukta 164, Verse 28-29

"Upon seeing the calf with closed eyes, the cow moos, the cow cleans the calf by licking its forehead and moos. Upon seeing the milk bubbles on the mouth of the calf, the cow moos. The cow feeds the calf with her milk.

The cow hears unspoken words of the calf, upon hearing which she surrounds the calf, and moos in the grazing pastures. Inspite of being an animal, the cow's intelligence exceeds that of human beings, and this manifests in her giving a huge quantity of milk."

It is also mentioned in the Samveda, that the *yajman* is desirous of imbibing the radiant qualities of gold, cow and knowledge of the truth. Thus, the cow was placed above humans, who sought to emulate her divine qualities.

यद्वर्चो हिरण्यस्य यद्वा वर्चो गवामुत

सत्यस्य ब्रह्मणो वर्चस्तेन मा स सृजामसि ॥

Samveda, Aranyak Parva, Chapter 6, Part 4, Verse 10

"The tejas present in gold, cows and the knowledge of truth is what we desire to receive."

"Tejas" refers to a certain type of life-giving energy.

In the Atharva Veda, the *rishis* pray for a long life of the cow to the devatas and mention their milk and *gobar* as divine items. They pray to be blessed with such cows and their calves.

संजग्माना अबिभ्युषीरस्मिन् गोष्ठे करीषिणीः

बिभ्रतीः सोम्यं मध्वनमीवा उपेतन ॥

"O cows! Please be in my goshala with your offspring, their offspring and be fearless of wild animals. Gobar giving and the one who removes diseases, and one who gives Amrit like milk, please bless me with your presence."

Atharva Ved, Sukta 14, Verse 3

The cow was also a symbol of wealth and prosperity, not just a domestic animal in the farm.

संवत्सरस्य प्रतिमां यां त्वा रात्र्युपास्महे

सा न आयुष्मतीं प्रजां रायस्पोषेण सं सृज ॥

Atharva Ved, Sukta 10, Verse 3

"O Night! You are the embodiment of the Samvatsaras. We worship you. Please bless our offspring and their offspring with a long life, and please bless us with cows and such wealth."

Agama texts go one step further. They mention the numerous ways in which the items obtained from the cow are sacred as well as directly applicable in everyday life, and what benefits they bring to the practioners.

Kamika Agama describes many types of sacred baths or *snaan*, which purify a person, of which the first is the *snaan* of the dust from the feet of the cow!

kuryāt gokulasaṁcāra dhūlibirvāyusambhavaiḥ |

puruṣeṇaiva mantreṇa snānānāṁ uttamottamam ||

Kamika Agama, Purva Pada, Chaper 3, Verse 104

"When the cows are moving about, the sadhaka should walk behind them and get himself bathed with the dusty particles raised by the wind from the feet of the cows. This should be done with the recital of tatpurusha mantra. This kind of bath is known as 'vayavya-snana' and this is considered to be the first and foremost kind of bath."

So not only the cow, or the items obtained from the cow, even the **dust flying from the feet of the cow is sacred**, and a purifier for human beings.

Bhasma, one of the most sacred items to Shaivites, is another item described in the Kamika Agama, along with its method of preparation and benefits to mankind. It is described as having the power to alleviate all types of diseases, and should be applied every day, in the form of "*bhasma snaan.*" This *bhasma,* is to be prepared from cow dung, along with the incantation of Shaiva *mantras,* also described in the Agama text.

bhuktimuktidaṁ āgneyaṁ kāryaṁ śuddhena bhasmanā ||

snānaṁ caturvidhaṁ bhasma bhavetkalpādi bhedataḥ |

kalpañcaivānukalpañca upakalpaṁ akalpakam ||

teṣvādyaṁ tata utkṛṣṭatamamanyadabhāvataḥ |

Kamika Agama, Purva Pada, Chapter 3, Verse 42-32

"The fiery bath is capable of yielding both the worldly enjoyments and the final liberation and it should be done with the sacred bhasma(vibhuti, holy ash). Based on the different varieties of bhasma such as kalpa and others, this fiery bath is considered to be of four types. Kalpa, anukalpa, upakalpa, akalpa – these are the four varieties of bhasma. Of these, kalpa is the most supreme. If kalpa is not available, other kinds of bhasma may be used."

Furthermore, Kamika Agama elaborately explains the method of preparation of the *panchagavya*, which is a combination of the five sacred items obtained from a cow. Every ritual starts with the purification of the land or the space, and this purification is done by sprinkling the *panchagavya*, and smearing the place with cow dung and/or cow urine by the *acharya* or *Guru* performing the ritual.

So, it is clear that the cow has been sacred to Hindus since the beginning of the civilization. Hinduism as a culture and religion is unique in the sense that it has both—the mutable and immutable aspects to it. So, while there are many aspects of the culture that change over a period of time, based on the demography, psychology and spiritual ambience of the people, there are certain aspects of Hinduism which are immutable and do not change, because they are founded on the eternal, timeless cosmic truths.

The 'S*hruti*' texts of Hinduism expound the immutable aspects of Hinduism. *Shrutis*—the Vedas and Agamas—are the scriptures directly captured as revealed by Mahadeva to the enlightened *Rishis*. Vedas give the pure science of Hinduism, and Agamas give the applied science – the lifestyle aspects. Together, Vedas and Agamas illumine humanity on the cosmic truths and how anyone can align their lives with these cosmic truths, through *yajna, puja, mantra, tantra, yoga, mudra,* and many other practices. The truths, methods, techniques given in the *Shruti* texts are the original, core tenets and practices of Hinduism which do not change over time. They are a capture of the Cosmos revealing itself to the *Rishi*. The *Smriti* texts are the knowledge-sharing of the *Rishis* and enlightened masters, some of which are complex Vedic sciences, experienced, experimented and explained by the *Rishis* of a *yuga* (era), for that *yuga*. Some aspects of it may change over a period of time, and some may not. *Itihaas* is the documented history of all beings that happened on the planet, in all the many dimensions. It describes incidents as they happened.

In all the three—Shruti, Smriti and Itihaas texts—cow is given an elevated place and considered worthy of worship and reverence for the divine qualities she possesses as a being. The kindness, innocence, and simplicity of the cow towards other creatures and her role in the human sphere as not just a pet animal, but a nurturer of the people she lives with, cannot be (The effects of positive human contact by tactile stimulation on dairy cows with different personalities 2018)undermined. She considers all who live with her as her family. Hence, the moniker, "mother cow" or "Gaumaata."

Modern Day Findings: Cow is a Sentient Being

What we know from Hindu scriptural texts is corroborated by findings of modern science. A study (Shahin, 2018) revealed that positive human contact improves the relationship between humans and cows. "High responder" and "low responder" cows both perceive the stroking equally. Another study (Pinheiro Machado et al., 2020) shows that cows regularly interact with each other and express affinity for each other through licking and proximity to preferred cows. Pregnant cows receive extra attention by way of extra licking by other cow-mates.

"The preferred companion lick each other more often and also fight more often."

Yet another study (A. Green et al., 2019) shows that cows talk to each other and show compassion just like human beings do. In this study, a team of scientists study the voice quality and vocalization of cows in different situations to arrive at conclusions about the sense of identity and empathy cows have. The lead researcher, Alexandra Green, says,

"They have all got very distinct voices. Even without looking at them in the herd, I can tell which one is making a noise just based on her voice." (Power of Positivity, 2020)

A previous study (Mónica Padilla de la Torre et al., 2016) demonstrated the sense of individuality conveyed by cows and calves while communicating with each other. This new study shows that cows maintain their individuality throughout their lives.

It makes sense that cows and calves maintain their close bonds as the calf is nursed by the cow. But the emotional bond between the cow and her calf is not severed ***even if the calf is not nursed by the cow.*** This study (Johnsen et al., 2015) demonstrates this observation in Holstein cows. On many dairy farms, calves are separated from their mothers at the time of birth and the mother cow is not allowed to nurse her baby calf. Yet, the emotional bond between them remains. Furthermore, it is seen(Flower & Weary, 2003) that calves who are nursed by their mothers grow up to be healthier, stand earlier and gain weight faster (at almost 3x the rate) than the calves who are reared on artificially limited supplies of milk.

Unfortunately, most of the available research has been done in countries which have higher populations of Holstein cows, and not the Indian *Bos Taurus*. But, a few of the cited studies include some *bos taurus* cows as well, and *the observations are the same in the two.*

Of course, those of us who have grown up with cows in India, would know these things from first-hand experience. Cows can be extremely protective of their calves in the midst of strangers, and not only this, they are also **protective of the human beings who nurture them every day.** They are sentient, gregarious creatures who nurture all beings who are a part of their "family."

The cow sees everyone who loves her as her family. She is, beyond doubts, ***a sentient being***.

The cow sees everyone who loves her as her family. She is, beyond doubts, ***a sentient being***.

A Quick Flashback

Cownomics is not a new concept. It is as old as time. Before learning how Cownomics can be used to address the challenges of the currently decrepit society, it is illuminating to get an unstinted perspective on ***what is an ideal, sustainable, healthy and functional society.*** This perspective may take many decades to be achieved, but it sets the benchmark of what we are aiming at.

To render this picture of a functional society built on Cownomics, we need not look forward alone. We need to rewind by a few centuries, back to the Vedic times, when Cownomics was the default setup of the society.

Objects in the Mirror Are Closer Than They Appear

The Indian farmer was not just a farmer. He was also a gopala – the one who takes care of cows. In the ancient Vedic age, every activity started and ended with a ritual and a yajna (fire ritual)– be it sowing the crops, harvesting crops or praying for crops.

In the Vedic times, in the Ganga Saraswati civilization, the oldest living civilization in the world, the farmers had intelligently integrated their farming practices with their daily duties and daily needs. They knew the ways to make a living and to run a life. When something did not work, they looked to the King, who in turn sought the counsel of the Rishis (seers) and Munis (sages) for solutions. The King was an enabler for countrymen, who helped them grow and prosper. Their prosperity was a thing of pride for the King. The King was expected to distribute daan or riches amongst the countrymen to fulfil their needs when required. The King was not the owner of wealth. He was the guardian of the wealth of the entire country. He, along with his ministers or "Mantri Mandal," was empowered to decide how to spend that wealth, or how to multiply it.

The cow played a central role in the Vedic society. No town or village was considered as "complete" without cows, because in the Vedic era, **the economy could not run without a cow!** In the Mahabharat, when the Pandavas move to Khandavprasth to start a new kingdom, they are given one lakh cows by Dhritrashtra to start their kingdom, despite the animosity between the two groups. The same cows later are stolen by Duryodhan, so as to prevent the Pandavas from performing the Rajsooya Yajna. Without cows, no important yajna could be performed. Hence, no event could be completed without cows. In the Kathopanishad, when King Vajashravas donates weak and ill cows during the yajna, his son Nachiketa offers himself as sacrifice in the yajna, to compensate for the inauthenticity of his father. So, it was important to take care of cows and make sure that they are strong and healthy.

The cow gave milk, gobar (cow dung) and gomutra (cow urine), each of which were utilized by the farmer in multiple ways. Milk was used for all cooking purposes, and further skimmed to get ghee, butter and curd. Milk, ghee (clarified butter), butter and curd were used not just in cooking, but also by Vaidyas (physicians) in preparing Aushadhis (remedies) for ailing people. Gobar was composted and used as manure to fertilize the field. So, there was no additional cost attached to fertilizing the land after multiple harvests. Gomutra mixed with herbs was sprinkled over the fields as a pesticide. Due to its unique qualities of killing pestilent insects, bacteria, weeds and virus, but not harmless plants, there was no additional burden of managing toxins and pollution. Gomutra was not poisonous by nature, and beneficial for humans too. This ensured that the gomutra sprinkled over crops did not alter the quality of food grown or turn it poisonous.

The food obtained from this organic farming (or just farming as it was back then) was nutritious, free of harmful chemicals and substances, and rich with life. It grew naturally, taking in the nutrition from the added manure, and the soil, and hence, had its own taste. The soil, because it was not overused or adulterated with chemicals, had its own qualities, which were added to the grown food, making the food everything a person would need to stay healthy. Food was medicine. No separate medicine was required to keep people healthy! *Aushadhis* used as medicine were meant for support in emergency situations. It was, essentially, a pill-free lifestyle. People did not take pills or medicines every other day, because the food made sure they received the right nutrients and herbs, so they did not fall sick as often or as much, and secondly, when they did, minor additions of herbs to everyday food could take care of the afflictions. *Aushadhis* helped in healing an aggravated condition which was an occasional occurrence.

When the cows walked all over the pastures and neighbouring lands and forests, they also deposited *gobar* at regular intervals, and also ploughed the soil with their hoofs. This made it easy for the manure to bind to the soil, and also for the soil to get pulverized and compacted both (due to the motion of hoofs), thus preventing it from erosion, and also giving it properties to absorb rainwater into the soil. Run off was minimized due to this combination of actions.

Oxen were used to plough the fields after harvest with a *"hal."* This removed additional cost of machinery for ploughing the fields. Oxen were also used to move grinding machines, where grains were ground into flour or oil squeezed from grains, thus no separate power source was required for the same.

Due to the insecticidal nature of both *gobar* and *gomutra*, a mixture of the two was used to plaster the walls of huts, so as to prevent infections and pests in the house. *Gobar* was also rolled into "cakes" or *"kapole"* or *"kande,"* which were then dried in the Sun. These dried cakes were used as fuel in the kitchen in the *angeethi* (stove). This eliminated the need to cut wood for cooking. Especially made *gobar* cakes were also used in *yajnas* as *ahuti* or offering in the *homa kunda*. Smaller parts of *gobar* were mixed with other herbs and dried in the Sun to create incense sticks which were used in *puja, yajnas* and other rituals, and doubled up as insect repellents.

Living with the cow, taking care of her and her family—oxen, calves etc.—created an ambiance of love and care for all the animals, and a natural inclination to live with animals and nurture them. When repeated over several generations, this created a default mental setup of nurturing cows and other animals rather than hurting or attacking them, unless they attack you, the latter of which were typically wild animals. The cow has a very deep emotional sense and is capable of very high levels of empathy and compassion. By living around her, children picked up the nature of compassion and empathy from childhood itself. What you learn in childhood as a part of "play" or recreation, stays with you much longer than any classroom lessons. Spending time with the cow was such a candid, recreational lesson. When children were sent to *gurukuls* (Vedic residential schools), their *acharya* (teacher) or Guru (Master) often gave them the task of looking after the cows and taking them out for grazing. **This was the practical lesson in empathy that children imbibed early on. They**

learnt kindness towards all living creatures by living with them and nurturing them.

Due to the love and affection showered on her, the cows gave a higher quantity of milk. When cows are happy and healthy, they naturally give a higher quantity of milk. They don't need to be medically treated for it at all. Thus, the circle of love between the *gau* and the *gopalas* had everlasting benefits for both.

This also involved the entire family—from the women, to the children, to the men, all had shared responsibilities. The burden of running the household did not rest on just one person. Each played their own role, and children learnt caring for the life of another being and taking responsibility at a very young age. When children start spending time thinking about living beings other than their own selves, their maturity starts. As long as a child is obsessed with only his/her entertainment or wish fulfillment, s/he remains a child. When s/he starts looking after others, s/he matures as a being. Living around the cow ensured that children developed the maturity needed to run any profession from a young age.

As everyone required the milk products in their daily lives, everyone either had a few cows, or bartered their goods with others in exchange for milk products. Milk, ghee, curd, butter were symbols of wealth and prosperity. Abundance of the same meant that you were blessed enough to have a profitably running venture. Having cows also gave a soft insurance from natural calamities like famines and droughts, since some trade could still run even if the crops go bad.

Every village and town followed the same cownomics model and was self-sustaining. It grew food, and other crops, and barter system or trade within the community made the cycle of trade going. No separate activity was required to create work, earning, living or to promote commerce. Every item of trade was either grown on the ground or obtained from the ground itself. Food, flowers, textiles were grown on the ground. Precious stones, earthenware were obtained from the ground. Architectural marvels were built on the ground. The merchants used their creativity to make items that were then sold, and the cycle of commerce continued. And *at the centre of all of it was the holy cow.*

Karmic Footprint & Carbon Footprint

There are two important, fundamental principles of Cownomics which will be used extensively in this book—the carbon footprint of every action, and the karmic footprint of every action. The former is commonly known to those with a scientific temperament, but the latter is as yet not known, nor popularly used. **"Karmic footprint" is a word I coined, to capture the essence of the karmic fall out of actions of individuals, as well as the society as a whole.**

Carbon Footprint

Carbon footprint is defined as:

> *"The total amount of greenhouse gases produced to directly and indirectly support human activities, usually expressed in equivalent tons of carbon dioxide." – timeforchange.org*

> *"Today, the term "carbon footprint" is often used as*

shorthand for the amount of carbon (usually in tonnes) being emitted by an activity or organization." – footprintnetwork.org

The carbon footprint of an activity is a yardstick to measure how much that activity is hurting the environment. An increase in the carbon footprint of any activity damages the environment, and directly affects the health and well-being of people. For example, carbon emissions from industrial areas or stubble burning by farmers, pollutes the air, giving people air borne allergies and respiratory diseases, thus deteriorating their health, sometimes irreparably. This is in addition to the fact that carbon emissions directly contribute to climate change as well. Climate change, in turn, speeds up the frequency of natural disasters, alters the climate irreparably, changes sea levels, changes the agricultural patterns of regions, and more.

Another related term is the "biocapacity" of any region.

"Biocapacity is the area of productive land available to produce resources or absorb carbon dioxide waste, given current management practices. Biocapacity is measured in standard units called global hectares." – footprintnetwork.org

Biocapacity is a way to estimate the capacity of a region to absorb atmospheric carbon emissions. The best way to remove carbon emissions is by agricultural, forestation and other such practices, which allow the carbon from the atmosphere to be absorbed back into the earth and green cover. Biocapacity is a measure of the same.

When the biocapacity of a region is outrun by its carbon footprint, it starts moving towards climate change as a region, and starts altering the environment.

Currently, **the biocapacity of India is 160% short of its carbon footprint** (*Open Data Platform*, 2021).

Only recently the government of India announced (Vishwa Mohan, 2018) that the sea levels along the coastline are expected to rise by 2.8 ft due to global warming and climate change. This has a far-reaching impact on the lives of many people. And, of course, it has a direct impact on the economy of the nation. Hence, the carbon footprint of any activity is, in one way or another, related to the economy of the country. The relationship may or may not be linear.

Karmic Footprint

The word "karmic footprint" of an activity is **a measure of the amount of violence, suffering or pain that action has caused to living beings.** Karma is the amount of suffering caused to any living being. Hence, the karmic footprint is a measure of the suffering caused. Since the impact is subjective, there is no clear objective way to measure the karmic footprint. Yet, its importance cannot be undermined. So, an ordinal scale, rather than a cardinal scale will be used to describe the karmic impact of different activities, as a decimal.

Anything which contributes to the economy materially, but eventually continues to cause suffering to people, causes violence, reduces the happiness and well-being of that demography, and again reduces their capacity to contribute to the society, cannot be thought of as making a positive contribution to the economy. This is less measurable as a direct metric than the carbon footprint of an activity, yet just as relevant. If you see your family crying every alternate day, would you be in your top form at your workplace? Probably not. That is the karmic footprint of an action. Anything that gives suffering to people, adversely affects the society as a whole, not just the people immediately involved. It may not be measurable in quantifiable ways, yet, it has an unmistaken impact on the overall economy. It impacts the mental, physical and spiritual well-being of people, and can be seen in their participation in the society.

In Cownomics, the economic impact of the carbon footprint and karmic footprint of all activities and changes has been considered.

Environment is Not "Outside"

When we think of the "environment," we think of something outside, something other than us. We think of it as the forests we rarely see, the mountains and rivers we visit on the summer break, and the innumerable organisms, whose names we don't know, and will likely never see in our lifetimes.

Everyone loves nature and wants to save the environment. But when we think of the environment, we think of this "other world" that exists beyond our daily lives, outside the ambit of our perceptions. We do not think of the cup of coffee on our desks, the handbag we carry with pride, the burrito we ate, the water we drink, the lanes we walk on, the people we meet, and the animals we feed. We subtract our immediate surroundings from our idea of the environment. We think saving the environment has to do with mass protests, sloganeering, Earth Day, Paris Climate Agreement, and our nation's policy on climate change. We subtract the chicken wings, eggs, sausages and beef steaks we partake of in every meal from our purview. Those chickens and pigs and cows were also once the environment—were, because now they are not. They were removed from the environment. By us. For a meal.

Yet not only is a human being the product of his/her environment, the "environment" is a product of his/her actions and decisions. And so on and so forth. It is a recursive loop, not a one-way street.

This "altered" environment directly affects us human beings in more than one way. It affects our bodies through the toxins we ingest, the miasmic air we breathe, the polluted water we drink. This chemically altered existence affects our mental health, and our capacity to rebound in the face of tragedy. That subtle thing called "will power" is not a magic ingredient in human beings. It is cultivated, not just with intensity, but with everyday life choices that ensure that we imbibe only what is the best for our body and minds. The word "natural" has so many meanings, yet human beings miss out the most important one: *as nature intended it to be.* And ingesting toxins, killing animals for just a snack, leaching off resources of the earth, wasting away bit by bit is not how nature intended us to be.

What does your meal cost?

India has, historically been an agrarian economy, and in the recent past, agriculture had a pivotal role to play in every major crisis in the world, directly or indirectly. Every war has changed the way we eat, and what we eat, for good or for worse. Animal agriculture, which was restricted to small animal farms, transmogrified into industrialized animal agriculture, in order to "optimize" constraints posed by small farms, allowing bigger corporations to step in and make heavy investments in new machinery and methods to confine animals and slaughter them as quickly as possible with the maximum output.

Industrial agriculture was believed to be an answer to the problems of shortage of food. Heavy mechanization of the farming sector, combined with chemical formulations to increase productivity promised a new world of abundance of food. Add to this a growing appetite for meat, met by industrialization of animal farms. The trend started in the western world, especially USA in the post-World War II world, but reached the rest of the world in no time.

The outcome? A lot more food, yes. But at what cost?

The statistics of meat consumption are mind boggling. Looking at the figures, even more concerning than the growing meat consumption is the reason (or reasons) for the same. What is making human beings eat so much meat? And what is it doing to us and the planet we all co-inhabit? That is a question I will keep going back to again and again throughout the length of this book. If there was ever a question with too many answers, it is that one.

Th average world meat consumption has grown manifold in the last half a century. Beef makes up a sizable part of this figure. Annual per capita meat consumption (world average) (Bill Winders & Elizabeth Ransom, 2019) was 20 kg in 1961. This increased by 50% to 30 kg by 1988, and doubled by 2013 to 40 kg. In roughly the same period (Hannah Ritchie & Max Roser, 2017), beef and buffalo meat production increased from 28 million metric tonnes (MMT) per year in 1961 to 68 MMT in 2014. At the same time, the population of the world grew from 3 billion in 1960 to 7 billion by 2016. So, the total meat consumption for the world roughly quadrupled in half a century!

This trend is not spread evenly across the world. There was a staggering growth in meat consumption in China and other Asian countries, correlated with economic growth in these

countries, whereas meat consumption in European countries showed a decreasing trend. Denmark, France and Netherlands saw a decreasing trend in meat consumption. Even Americans showed a declining rate of meat consumption till 2014, only to pick it back up again. Yet, the effect of increased "meatification" of foods in Asia more than cancelled out the effect of meat cutbacks in Europe and USA. China's meat production increased from 2.55 million metric tonnes in 1961 to 88.16 million metric tonnes in 2018. China increased its meat production by almost 35 times. It also became a leading exporter and consumer of meat, overtaking the market share for meat in the global meat industry.

Where does meat come from?

The sharp increase in the figures for meat production and consumption can sometimes obfuscate the grim reality behind those figures: where does this growing supply of meat come from? From slaughtered animals, ofcourse.

"In 2018, an estimated 69 billion chickens; 1.5 billion pigs; 656 million turkeys; 574 million sheep; 479 million goats; and 302 million cattle were killed for meat production." - Our World in Data

That's **72.511 billion animals slaughtered in one year,** making their way to our plates. That is roughly ten times the total human population on the planet. How hungry can we get?

We have ravaged the earth to fill our plates, not heeding what it does to the world outside of our bubbles. Maybe we need to stop and ponder: where are all these animals coming from? Surely, this is not a normal reproductive rate. Animals do not breed at this rate on their own. They are the product of a system that exists solely to multiply the numbers of animals at the highest rate possible. For chickens, that rate is much higher, hence the number of chickens we eat per year has grown more than that of other animals: logistically, they take less space, need less time to grow, can become meat faster. Other animals, like cows take more space, need more time to become beef, hence cost of rearing them is higher.

Cows are forced to reproduce constantly through artificial insemination. It weakens their bodies and shortens their natural lifespan. They are forced to constantly lactate, to supply milk to the dairy industry. On industrial dairy farms, their calves are often separated from them at the time of birth. They are forced to go on giving birth to calves without getting to even see their baby after giving it birth. Many of these calves are slaughtered shortly after their birth to become the veal that is considered a "delicacy" by much of the European world. Many calves are fitted with devices on their mouths which have spikes, so that if they go to the mother to drink her milk, she will be caused immense pain and have no option but to push the calf away. These are devices to ensure a consistent supply of milk and beef to the world which is forever hungry.

Human beings have intervened in the reproductive cycles of animals and forced them to reproduce and multiply at exorbitantly high rates, through cruel methods, seeing animals solely as a source of protein or milk, and not as living beings born on this earth to live their own lives.

A Disbalance in Nature

The earth is not just a land mass with water patches. It is a living thing. It grows, it expands, it contracts, it evolves, it changes. It is a dynamically changing thing, which allows millions of life forms to survive on it. As the atmosphere and overall natural environment changes due to natural effects (although it is tough to differentiate which effects are "natural" now since humans have found a way to meddle with every aspect of nature!), the earth also evolves to make the change possible and feasible. Through the numerous ice ages, the atmosphere of the earth changed drastically, leading to new life forms, and making some life forms like the famous dinosaurs extinct. These were natural phenomena. As the clime around the earth changes on its own, the earth, which is a living organism, evolves to create a new ecosystem which it can support.

But what happens if there are drastic changes in a very short span of time, which completely disbalance the existence of life forms on earth? The earth will not have the means to support those changes. If, instead of 10 billion animals, we exponentially, and artificially increase that number to ~70 billion animals in just 60 years' time, it is too drastic and asymmetric a change which the earth cannot adapt to so quickly. Combined with this, there is a drastic decrease in forest cover and wildlife. This means that the elements which the earth was self-architected for are in a very different proportion today from what they were a very short time ago. When we think of the evolution that happened during the ice ages, 60 years is a very short time.

The earth has not had sufficient time to adapt to those changes, and the disbalanced load on all the forces of nature is pushing humanity towards calamities of all types, most of which are going unnoticed and unheeded. Even as we speak, our soils are losing fertility and getting eroded, our waters are getting polluted, possibly even poisoned, the air we breathe is getting more toxic, the ocean levels are rising, the ice caps are melting faster, the rivers are getting dirtier, the lakes are frothing with waste, the oceans are more turbulent, there are islands of plastic waste, the seasons are moving towards extremes, and we have more frequent epidemics and pandemics. This is not the outcome of some paranoid reasoning. Yes, we always had natural disasters and epidemics and pandemics. But the rate at which we have disturbed the ecological balance of the earth is not the same. The result will not be the same. The frequency, intensity and mystery around calamities will be higher, since we have not had enough time to even study a lot of the phenomena we started! Outright denial of the problem is one more aspect of the problem.

The Earth will not thank you

A lot of times, when we are asked if that steak or the chicken wings are "worth it," the prompt answer is, "of course!" Let us take a look at what 1kg of meat is really worth. What is the cost at which we obtain it?

> *"If all the grain currently fed to livestock in the United States were consumed directly by people, the number of people who could be fed would be **nearly 800 million**," David Pimentel, professor of ecology in Cornell University's College of Agriculture and Life Sciences (U.S. Could Feed 800 Million People with Grain That Livestock Eat, Cornell Ecologist Advises Animal Scientists | Cornell Chronicle, 1997)*

Animal protein is got via a longish route, as far as sources of energy go. For each animal which is slaughtered and converted into meat, it needs to be fed grains and/or forage in its lifetime to fatten it and keep it alive. This feed may or may not be grown in the same place where animals are reared. In most of the concentrated feeding operations (CAFOs), the feed is transported from some other location. To grow this feed requires natural resources like land, water, soil nutrients, and manual labour or mechanical tilling and harvesting. It could also be dependent on the seasons and subject to the vagaries of local microclimates. Every aspect of this supply chain sucks resources out of the earth, and at the far end of it is your plate, with the proteinaceous meal you look forward to. Behind the plate is a curtain which obliterates everything else that goes into bringing that meal to you. Everything else happens "backstage," so to speak.

How much food does your food require?

As of 2003, as per the noted ecologist David Pimentel (Pimentel & Pimentel, 2003) the US livestock population consumed as much as seven times the quantity of grains consumed by the entire American population. The amount of grains which are fed to livestock reared by the meat industry in USA, would be **sufficient to feed 840 million more people,** were they to stick to a purely plant-based diet.

In the midst of the political cacophony on rising inequality, poverty and resource constraints, there lies a tiny solution if the world chose to take it: eating plant-based. If all the meat-eaters ate less meat, more people can be fed. The entire population of Africa, the continent, is 1.2 billion. Of those 1.2 billion, an estimated 440 million people live below poverty line (as reported in 2019) (Kristofer Hamel et al., 2019). 1/5th of the African (*Poverty in Africa: Facts & Figures - SOS Children's Villages USA*, n.d.) population is considered to be malnourished—the largest proportion in the world. Imagine what the world would look like if 840 million of those 1.2 billion people could be fed, taking care of the most vital human requirement of food for all those below poverty line in Africa. And this is based on the statistics for USA alone. If an equivalent calculation was done for the world, it is quite possible that all the people below poverty line in the world could be fed and would not have to starve to death. As per an estimate by Kearney (*When Consumers Go Vegan, How Much Meat Will Be Left on the Table for Agribusiness? - Kearney*, n.d.), based on the world population of 2018, we would have food for an additional 7 billion people if everyone switched to a plant-based diet. A world without hunger! Imagine that.

For the production of 1 kCal of beef, about 40 kCal of fossil energy is used up. The ratio is different for different animals, with beef and lamb taking the top spots. Egg follows next with a 39:1 ratio. The average fossil energy ratio is 25:1 for all animal protein. This is more than 11 times the ratio for grain protein production, which stands at 2.2 kCal of fossil energy used for 1 kCal of plant protein produced, taking corn as an example (the ratio may vary for other plant-based sources of protein).

Growing usage of fertilizers, pesticides and mechanization in agriculture and livestock means that these industries are acutely dependent on fossil fuels. The fossil fuel reserves of the earth are dwindling and are slated to disappear in the next few decades. The jury is still out on the exact year for this, but it is safe to say that we are headed for a world with zero fossil fuels. While the climate scientists argue over how much fossil fuels we have left, we can't keep guzzling fossil fuels as if there's no tomorrow. But we are doing precisely that. Fertilizers and pesticides production guzzle energy from fossil fuels. The Haber Bosch process used for manufacturing synthetic Nitrogen fertilizers is extremely energy intensive and uses natural gas. Phosphorus and Potassium fertilizer plants use electricity, most of which is derived from fossil fuels. Pesticides are created from petrochemicals, and again, use up huge energy resources. Irrigation, tilling, harvesting, milking the cattle, refrigeration, all require either electricity or fuel. In the USA, food travels an average of 2400 km before it is consumed. This is obviously energy intensive. Apart from the costs to the environment, this is an important factor in determining the stability of the industry. As fossil fuels disappear, food is likely to get more expensive, and prices likely to be more volatile. What happens to the food for the poor then? The food supply will be limited by availability of fuels. A big part of agriculture is pastureland or land for growing feed for livestock. This is an additional, unnecessary burden on the fuel demands of a country.

A plant-based diet, though frowned upon by meat eaters, provides not only the same calorific value, but even the same nutrients as a meaty diet, if the right mix of crops is grown for food. It takes 7 kg of feed grain to produce 1 kg of live weight for cows. So, if someone who eats beef went plant-based, not only would they eat a lot more for lesser natural resource consumption, but they would have the same nutrients, and not have to kill a cow for it.

Where does your food live?

In a world where human population and the livestock population continue to grow at an alarming rate, the available arable land is, effectively, shrinking. A prime problem of forcing animals to reproduce as fast and as much as possible is that it requires space. The animals need to eat, and growing their food requires space too. The arable land available to us is limited, getting more and more limited. Our requirements are increasing, while at the same time, arable land is decreasing. The combined effect is manifold.

The problem of land degradation can be understood by many routes. But the destination is always the same. If we have no land, we have no food. No matter how much science grows foods in labs, and how much we engineer plants, we will still not have enough food to feed all the humans on this planet if we keep eating meat at the same rate, and keep destroying soil at the same rate—and both these activities are closely inter-related, as we are about to see. At the risk of sounding alarmist, cutting back on meats is the only way in which we can make sure we don't have a much, much hungrier world a decade down the line.

> *"Industrial meat is the fastest-growing form of meat production and consumption in the world."—Mindi Schneider (Schneider, 2014)*

The industrialization of the meat industry meant heavy mechanization, and increasing reliance on feed crops: maize, soya bean and oil seeds. This meant monoculture fields—fields with only one crop—and packed "prisons" for animals. It destroyed any bio-diversity that had been historically preserved in the fields and in livestock. These economies of scale give a very acceptable delusion of cost reduction for meat on the surface, but hide the sordid reality of animal cruelty, land degradation and resource depletion. The profits from the industry hide heavy costs as externalities. Subsidies given to the meat industry exacerbate the problem. The method used to cloud over these problems are *"biophysical overrides"* as described by Tony Weis (Weis, 2013).

Growing the same crops repeatedly on the same patch of land depletes the soil of nutrients: this is a serious concern in areas where feed is grown, since the same crop is sown over and over again. Inorganic fertilizers add back some of the minerals to the soil, but they cannot make up for the loss of organic matter from the soil. **Soil is a microbiome**. It is full of bio-diversity. It is home to numerous organisms, insects, worms, and organic matter which all, together, make the soil fertile and self healing. Chemical fertilizers do not make the soil "fertile." They simply add some of the chemicals back to the soil—they replace the depleted nitrogen, phosphorus, and potassium. The problems of weeds are overridden by inorganic pesticides. But the combination of pesticides and inorganic fertilizers also destroy much of the microbiome of the soil. This means that the top soil is getting depleted too fast for anyone to replenish it in their lifetimes.

"From 1961 to 2009, the area devoted to maize increased by 50 percent and the area devoted to soybeans more than quadrupled, while the area devoted to most other feed crops was relatively stagnant." - Tony Weis (Weis, 2013).

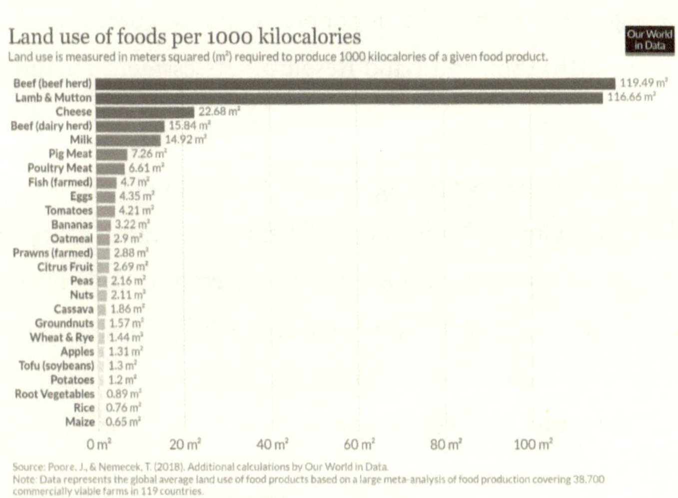

As of 2014 (Schneider, 2014), 57% of the world's barley, rye, millet, oats and maize were fed to industrial livestock. In the US, 44% of the country's maize is fed to livestock, and in the EU,

45% of wheat is for livestock. As per estimates of UN, 70% of the world's cultivated land is related to livestock production, while one third is directly related to growing livestock feed.

In the small farms that allow for "grass-fed" meats, there's the problem of over-grazing. Cows, sheep and buffalos have very little area to graze on, and could lead to over-grazing problems, once again degrading soil at a rapid rate.

As per a report by AT Kearney (*When Consumers Go Vegan, How Much Meat Will Be Left on the Table for Agribusiness? - Kearney*, n.d.), in 1970, the ratio of humans to arable land was around 0.38 hectares per head. By 2050, this is projected to decline to 0.15 hectares. Per Capita arable land in India, which is around 0.15 ha at present, is expected to decrease to a meager 0.09 ha by 2075, as per projections of government of India (2016) (Soil and Land Resources Assessment Division, 2016).

Classified based according to the International Monetary Fund and United Nations classification, the least developed economies experienced the highest prediction of soil erosion rate in 2001 (4.81 Mg/ha/ yr), equal to 4.8 Pg /yr and 13.6% of the global soil erosion. - An assessment of the global impact of 21st century land use change on soil erosion (Borrelli et al., 2017).

Each year about 90% of US cropland loses soil at a rate 13 times above the sustainable rate of 1 ton/ha/y. US pastures and rangelands are losing soil at an average of 6 tons/ha/y. About

60% of United States pastureland is being over-grazed and is subject to accelerated erosion.

In India, soil is eroded at an average annual rate of 16.35 tons per hectare per year which means 5334 million tons per year for the country as a whole, as per estimates from 1983. This is equivalent to 1 mm loss of topsoil per year. As per a report by the IPCC, soil erosion from agricultural fields is estimated to be 10 to 20 times (no tillage) to more than 100 times (conventional tillage) higher than the soil formation rate. The area of drylands has increased by 1% every year, in the period from 1961 to 2013.

> *"Growth is particularly pronounced in so-called developing countries, where governments and firms are keen to use meat as a new source of profit and legitimacy."—Schneider 2013*

The time required to replace approximately 1 inch of topsoil is 500 years. None of us is going to see this topsoil replaced during our lifetimes. Once it's gone, it's gone, for all intents and purposes.

When land is degraded, it stops binding water in it, allowing higher run off. When the run off is higher, soil is eroded faster. It is a cyclical and severe problem, which often does not find any mention in any policy or discussion, even though it could lead to no food for people very soon.

The loss of top soil is not just an environmental problem, it is a severe economic problem and has huge economic implications. With degradation of land, its utility diminishes rapidly, rendering it useless for most feasible purposes. If land gets desertified due to loss of vegetation and erosion, it has an impact on the micro-climate and on climate change overall. It can affect local temperatures, change rainfall patterns, and affect harvests even in the land that *is cultivable*. Most of agriculture depends on timely rainfall, especially in developing countries. Alteration in rainfall patterns can lead to one whole crop going bad, leading to poverty, hunger, famines and economic losses to the country.

The FAO led Global Soil Partnership[20] reports that 75 billion tonnes (Pg) of soil are eroded every year from arable lands worldwide, which equates to an estimated financial loss of US$400 billion per year (Borrelli et al., 2017).

Loss of organic matter adds to the burdens of depleted top soil by also making it difficult to bind carbon dioxide from the atmosphere to the ground. The soil microbiome has the capacity to hold a lot of carbon, which is converted from the CO_2 in the atmosphere by its organisms. With the heavy spray of herbicides and insecticides, these organisms no longer exist. Excessive tillage and over-grazing destroy green cover of the soil. Thus, a lot of the CO_2 that could potentially have been sequestered into the soil, will not be. Outcome will be an increase in the atmospheric load of CO_2.

The destruction of nature's resources was never going to be good news.

Meat itself was a menace because of the cruelty meted out to animals and the unhealthy lifestyles it promotes. But industrialization and rapid, mindless growth in the consumption and production of meat has made this menace a hundred times worse. The externalities of this industry have gone largely ignored, and it does not get the bad rap it should for not just destroying animals and human health, but the very land we need to survive on this planet, the very water we need to drink. This obsession with meat is irrational, and driven by twisting the supply-demand of the industry through subsidies, heavy advertising and promotion of meats, and the sector getting organized through mechanization and industrialization of agriculture. The meat industry is heavily controlled by a few top tier companies in the USA and Europe, who supply the lion's share of meat to the world. The small farmer, even in this "efficient" setup, does not make profits anywhere close to what the meat giants do, in USA. So it then adds to one more societal problem: that of inequality.

Water Hoofprint of your food

Water is life. Water is not the source of life, ***it is life***. Human beings are more than 80% water. From a single cell organism to the most evolved species, without water, there is no life. When we look for life on other planets, we look for water. The Earth is called the Blue Planet because of water. To destroy water is to destroy life itself.

Every year, a new city in India runs out of water. Be it Shimla or Chennai, the problem remains that India has now started facing severe water shortages, and has little by way of solution other than rain water harvesting. We are not yet looking at the grassroot problem of water shortage: why did we run out of water in the first place? If these cities have survived alright for hundreds of years, perhaps even thousands of years, why this sudden shortage? *What are we doing wrong?*

Many people are working on solving the problem of water scarcity through better water management, rainwater harvesting, reviving rivers and lakes and so on and so forth.

But the biggest culprit in the equation gets invariably overlooked, both, in activism as well as in policy making: **meat and dairy industry, and their cousin, the leather industry.**

The meat, leather and dairy industry the world over rely on water for numerous aspects of the meat/dairy/leather production cycle. From irrigation of the crops grown as feed to the animals' drinking water, to cleaning the animal shelters or CAFOs, sanitation of farms, to processing of meat, dairy or leather, every part of the process involves water consumption.

Agriculture accounts for 92% of the freshwater footprint of humanity; almost one third relates to animal products (Gerbens-Leenes et al., 2013).

There are different types of "waters" based on the usage and availability of water. Blue water refers to the water in rivers and lakes, and fit for human consumption. Green water is rainwater, minus run off. Grey water is the amount of water required to absorb pollutants released by a process. The total water footprint (Arjen Y. Hoekstra et al., 2011) considers all three in the calculation.

Of all types of meat production, beef has the largest water footprint, and consistently so in all countries. Producing 1 kilogram of industrial beef requires 15,415 liters of water (on average), mostly in the form of 'virtual water' used in the process of feed production. Among countries, India has a much larger water footprint for beef production than any

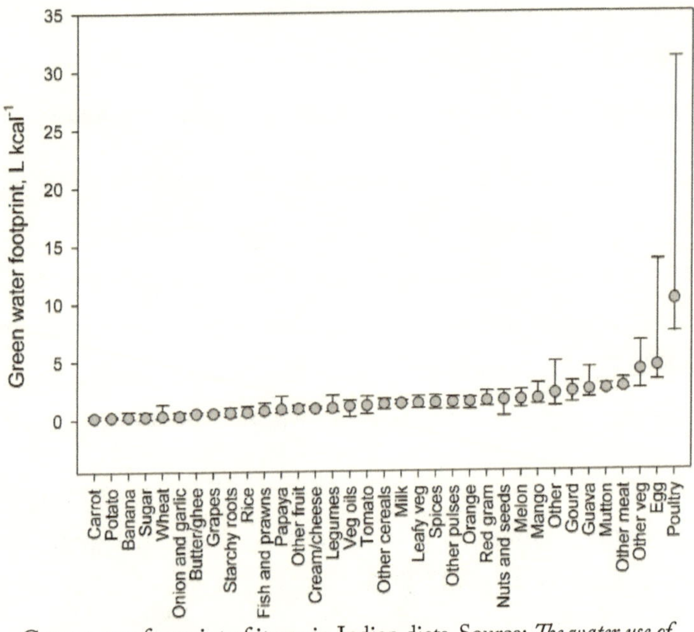

Green water footprint of items in Indian diets. Source: *The water use of Indian diets and socio-demographic factors related to dietary blue water footprint* (Harris et al., 2017)

other major economy, including China and USA. The weighted average green water footprint for beef production is 15,537 m3/ton in India, whereas it is 12,795 m3/ton in China and 12,933 m3/ton in USA. This is attributed to agricultural practices that are more water consumptive than other countries.

"When we consider the total water footprint per animal category, we find that beef cattle have the largest contribution (33%) to the global water footprint of farm animal production, followed by

dairy cattle (19%), pigs (19%) and broiler chickens (11%)."—A Global Assessment of the Water Footprint of Farm Animal Products (Mekonnen & Hoekstra, 2012).

In India, where 90% of freshwater is used in agriculture, this has serious implications. It means that if we don't change our eating patterns really soon, the imminent water crisis, which is caused largely by our food, will be that much sooner and worse.

India also has the highest green water footprint for leather production, resting at 15,103 m^3/ton. The average total water footprint for the world for leather is 17,093 m^3/ton. This is equivalent to 17,093 liters of water required for production of 1 kg leather. Assuming that a human being drinks 2 liters of water per day, the amount of water required to produce 1 kg leather would last one person 8546 days or roughly 24 years of their life. So, buying a fancy handbag that weighs half a kg is equivalent to wasting water that could have been drunk for 12 years!

Vegetables have a low water footprint of around 300 m3/ton. So, for every 1 kg of beef produced, 51 kgs of vegetables could be produced, using the same quantity of water.

This is the price paid for every kg of beef or leather sold on the market. The cost is an externality borne by all who are a part of the entire supply chain, and hence is not easily calculated in monetary terms, but it is evident where the water scarcity problem is coming from. It is a grey area that gets conveniently overlooked by all, since the bulk of the water consumption is in the feed and sanitation aspect of the production cycle, and not directly linked with meat, dairy or leather industry in a visible way.

"Meat-based diets have a larger water footprint compared to a vegetarian diet. We explored the implications of our results by examining the diet within one developed country—the USA—to determine the effect of diet composition on water footprint. Meat contributes 37% towards the food-related water footprint of an average American citizen. Replacing all meat by an equivalent amount of crop products such as pulses and nuts will result in a 30% reduction of the food-related water footprint of the average American citizen." - A Global Assessment of the Water Footprint of Farm Animal Products (Mekonnen & Hoekstra, 2012)

The damage done by this triad—meat, dairy and leather industries—is no longer a matter that can be ignored, since it has come to light that a lot of the droughts and water crises in the world can now be linked back to this triad, and there is a need for governments to intervene urgently to ensure that we can still survive with some water to drink every day. A recent drought in California, followed by restrictions in usage of water, led to some policy reckoning on this matter. A study

(Richter et al., 2020) on the subject showed that bad irrigation practices, which are linked to animal agriculture, are at the bottom of this crisis. A similar result was found for the Colorado basin, where rivers are getting depleted, causing damage to aquatic life and lowering of water level of Lake Meade. Cattle feed crops were found to be the largest consumptive user at both regional and national level, making up for 23% of all water consumption nationally in USA, and 55% of the water consumed in the Colorado River basin. Further, the study states that cattle feed crops are the leading cause of water depletion in a big chunk of western USA, accounting for roughly 75% of water used in the 369 sub-watersheds.

It is estimated that almost two-thirds of the water from the western USA rivers ends up as beef and the remaining is used up by dairy products. So, the triad shoulders the responsibility of water depletion in western USA squarely (Troy Farah, 2020).

But that's not it. Meat companies in USA (ANNA STAROSTINETSKAYA, 2019)are discharging waste into the Gulf of Mexico at an unprecedented rate. Mighty Earth, an environmental organization, found that the top meat companies discharge approximately 220 million tons of pollutants, the equivalent of almost 500 times the waste created by the city of New York, per year. Unlike human waste, waste from meat companies is not required to be treated before being discharged into water bodies. Due to the high consumption of water during the meat manufacturing process, most of these companies are located along the waterways. Every summer, this discharge of waste causes a hypoxic "dead swamp" or a toxic swamp in the Gulf of Mexico, where the oxygen levels in the water fall so low that aquatic life cannot survive. This is expected to worsen with an increase in the demand for food.

If we don't have a lot of food, we can eat less and still survive. But what will we do when we don't have water? Is it worthwhile to feast on beef steaks, at the expense of other people or even your own self running out of water?

Poisoning the Water, Earth and Air, One Field at a Time

Apart from the damage done to the environment by the animal agriculture industry, there is an additional load on the environment from agriculture itself—because of unbridled usage of chemical pesticides. The growth of animal agriculture has led to a boom in agriculture as well, because of increased demands for livestock and animal feeds. A lot more food is now needed, and crops must give higher yields, somehow, to feed the growing number of animals. So, vegetation cover must be cleared to make fields and fields must give higher yields. Moreover, with growing human population, there is a higher demand for food. Since a lot of existing agricultural land is getting converted to land for feeds, there is additional pressure on farmers to grow human foods in higher quantity as well.

Yields, yields, yields = money, money, money. That's the argument.

Chemical pesticides are toxic substances meant to kill insects, organisms, weeds and any kind of "pest" which would damage a crop, reducing yields. While the idea sounds noble and efficient, there is one snag: chemical pesticides are poisonous, and food should not be grown around poisons. Food and poison don't go together.

In reality, chemical pesticides can poison the air, water, soil, grass, vegetation and crops, and have adverse effect on other organisms in the soil, birds, insects which are not harmful (like bees and butterflies), fish, and scores of other flora and fauna who may not even be the target of the pesticides. We must account for (David Pimentel, 2001) almost 10 billion non target organisms, potentially at risk from a total of 700 or more chemical pesticides used in the world. Humans, of course, do not escape this net. Due to pollution of the soil, water and food supply, chemical pesticides make their way to our digestive tracts, and come in contact with our skins, and trigger diseases and numerous complex conditions in human beings. Chemical pesticides are pollutants which affect every aspect of life, even though they remain invisible and ignored. Only **0.1%** of pesticides reach their target; rest are left as residues in the environment (Pimentel et al 1992; Carriger et al 2006). That's a whole lot of pesticides we are talking about.

Pollution of the environment is only one step preceding direct harm to human beings—it invariably leads to chemical pesticides entering the food chain. In a study performed in West Bengal (Kole et al., 2001), India, the largest consumer of inland fish, the researchers discovered that a whopping percentage of fish samples had residues of chemical pesticides in them, a big number of which were way above the legal limit of acceptable content. The Earth's aquatic life is getting severely affected by the runoff from fields, making its way into aquifers and water bodies. Several studies have shown how aquatic life can be affected by water pollution. But that is only the tip of the iceberg. What about all the water bodies which have not been tested? Which is the bulk of the water systems. How do we know that the water being used somewhere is not coming from a water source that is contaminated? We don't—unless we know that the entire region has taken to organic farming, like Sikkim or Bhutan. Water can travel across great distances. So it is not right to assume that only the region where pesticides are sprayed will be affected. With crops like rice, which require flooding of fields, there is little chance that spraying of pesticides will *not* cause widespread water contamination. That rice, and that water, can find its way to our plates in myriad ways. This is not an alarmist argument, this is reality. This is not hypothetical, this is happening. This is not a scary future, this is the dismal state of the present.

Everything is connected to everything. Toxic water in the ground kills organisms in the soil, leading to damage to the soil, thus destroying the capacity of the soil to regenerate itself. **Soil is a microbiome. An estimated 4.5 tons/ ha of fungi and bacteria live in the topsoil (top 15 cm).** By indiscriminate use of chemical pesticides—like spraying them all over the fields with the use of drones and other such equipment—the microbiome is under threat. It is dying or spiraling into wrong patterns of growth. When the soil loses its ability to "recharge" itself, to digest organic matter and convert it to nutrients, to fix nitrogen from the atmosphere, the soil slowly becomes more and more barren, and dependency on inorganic fertilizers gets higher and higher. Inorganic fertilizers once again cause immense damage to the environment and are bad news for health. This also accelerates our loss of topsoils. Soils which do not have organic matter are more prone to getting eroded and causing high run off of rainwater. So, we lose ground water faster as well, over time. The ground water we do have, of course, is also getting contaminated. Some scientists estimate that at least one half of the ground water in USA already is, or is highly likely to be contaminated (Holmes et al.) Then there is the high cost of cleanup of this ground water, which is largely seen as an isolated issue, rather than linked with pesticide usage, where the blame rightly belongs. That cost never gets plugged into cost-benefit equation of pesticides.

It triggers a vicious cycle, which keeps feeding on itself, unless we make a conscious shift and move towards ecologically sound solutions which consider the impact of our actions on all creatures and organisms. As is obvious, our actions which are insensitive to other organisms, eventually bring the toxicity we dole out back to our own selves, in one way or another. The poison we spray out there for other creatures to die finds its way into our own bodies. Its a karmic cycle. It keeps repeating ad infinitum, unless we put a hard stop, and make a permanent change, not minor tweaking of the way we address the problem.

As per Dr David Pimentel (David Pimentel, 2001), in the USA, approximately 35% of all foods have pesticide residues, and at least 1-3% of all foods have residues higher than the FDA allowed limits. In contrast, in India, 97.5% of all foods have pesticide residues and 25% of foods have residues above the tolerance limits. This statistic is from 2001. As of 1990, in the USA (Pimentel et al., 1992), approximately 0.5 million tons of pesticides were used per year, at an annual cost of 4.1 Billion USD. But the most remarkable fact is that in spite of such heavy use of pesticides, pests destroyed 37% of crops per year. Even with a tenfold increase in pesticide use from 1945 to 1989, the percentage of crops destroyed by pests only *increased* from 7% to 13%. This involves questionable agricultural practices, and a lack of understanding of agriculture itself. Reports which highlight the benefits of pesticides, by increasing crop yields, grandly ignore the severe externalities, accompanying bad practices which are inefficient, and are in no way indicative of the overall benefits and drawbacks of pesticides. It is a flawed calculation.

As per statistics from 1992, the leading reason for poisoning in domestic pets like dogs and cats was pesticide poisoning. As per reports (Pimentel et al., 1992), nearly 40% of all the 25,000 calls for poisoning made to Iowa Animal Poison Control Center in 1987 were due to pesticide poisoning. This figure could be considerably higher today, considering the growth of pesticide use by leaps and bounds, but we do not have the corresponding data. Meat, eggs and dairy are also contaminated—to what extent, we don't know because not sufficient investigation has been done in this area. But it would make sense since the feed given to animals in animal farms is grown using pesticides. The water they drink is not necessarily treated for pesticide contamination. As per estimates, 30 million USD was lost (Pimentel et al., 1992) due to pesticide poisoning of domestic animals in USA. This is an indicative figure. It is difficult to hazard a guess on what this figure would be, were we to take losses in animal agriculture into account. Of course, economic losses are not the only criterion, and loss of life is a tragedy beyond just money, but the economic losses do need to be plugged into the cost-benefit equation for the usage of chemical pesticides.

As of 1992 (Pimentel et al., 1992), out of the 600 pesticides being used in USA, only 42 were tested in meat and eggs by the testing agency—National Residue Program. Moreover, by the time they released test results, the meat was already sold on the market. So, though there is no direct "economic loss" to the animal agriculture industry, there would definitely be a loss to consumers, who would have developed health issues due to the contaminated meat and eggs, which will go unaccounted for, and never get added to the cost-benefit equation of chemical pesticides. This is why the increased yields from pesticide usage look justified: because we are using the wrong equation to calculate its benefits. As of 1987, approximately 3% of the chicken sold in the market in USA had pesticide residues above the tolerable threshold.

One aspect of agriculture, grossly ignored by modern day farmers, is that "pests" have natural enemies, which keep their population under control. Organisms eat other organisms. It is nature's way of keeping balance in the Universe, which does not need to be interfered with. Whenever humans have interfered with nature's natural patterns, they have only created more problems for themselves as well as the whole eco-verse. Chemical pesticides are one such example. Excessive usage of chemical pesticides destroys not just pests, but the enemies of pests too, leading to a sudden boom in pest population, which is even more difficult to control, and a bigger problem than before because the natural enemies are now fewer. It leads to pest outbreaks. This is true for insects as well as fungi and other organisms. Nature has prey and parasites in myriad forms, and many such linkages may even be unknown to humans, or to farmers at any rate. Indiscriminate spraying of pesticides destroys organisms which were good for the crops. Sometimes, this also leads to *additional pests*, for which *more pesticides* are sprayed. It is estimated that 520 million USD are spent on additional usage of pesticides due to this mismanagement of pest control via pesticides.

Though such cases abound, one famous example is the case of Indonesia. From 1980-85, the usage of pesticides in Indonesia led to such a massive outbreak of pests that they recorded an all-time low yield of rice and had to import rice—a first for Indonesia which is an exporter of rice! They recorded losses to the tune of 1.5 billion USD (FAO 1988).

The cost-benefit equation of chemical pesticides is beginning to look more and more bleak. The cost side is weighing it down.

The one aspect of all life forms that humans consistently ignore is their ability to adapt to surroundings—which humans often lack. We try to deform the surroundings as per our needs and requirements, rather than trying to adapt. But that is not the way of nature. Every life form is endowed with enough intelligence for it to transform, change itself, even biologically, to survive and adapt to changing surroundings. So, when humans relentlessly spray pesticides on fields, the organisms living there, over a period of time, adapted, and developed resistance to pesticides. They stopped dying from pesticides. That's a checkmate move which humans did not see coming. After spraying tons of pesticides and poisoning everything from the air and water to the food we eat, humans discovered that the pesticides had little effect on pests (insects, weeds, plant pathogens) after a few years. So, it was all in vein after all. As per the work of Dr Pimentel, as of 1992, there were 504 insect and mite species, 150 plant pathogens and 273 weeds which had developed resistance to pesticides.

This has often led to the abandonment of an entire crop, because there was no way to save it. An example from Mexico in 1970: 250,000 hectares of cotton crop had to abandoned because the insects had developed resistance to pesticides sprayed. A study (Carrasco-Tauber 1989) showed that California clocked losses in the range of 45-120 per hectare of crop in 1989 due to pesticide resistance of pests, totaling to 348 million $ of losses. Taking the losses as 10% of total crop - which was the case in California - as representative for the country, to arrive at an estimate, the losses due to pesticide resistance could be as high as 1.2 billion $ per year for USA.

If this isn't enough wreckage to reckon with, and pesticides still look good, let me point out the crop damage due to the loss of bee populations—if bees die many crops don't get properly pollinated and hence, the yield is not good. Additionally, there are losses due to damaged crops from leftover pesticides of previous crops in the soil, which are toxic to the next crop rotation, and the ever -growing damages to human life, which are explored in far more detail in a later chapter. Adding all of these to the cost-benefit equation will give a very different picture of the methodology.

The only thing that remains surprising is that many people are still completely unaware of the negative aspects of pesticides, or stubbornly refuse to acknowledge them, because it does not fit a certain worldview of "scientific progress" leading the way to growth for human beings. The idea that nature and indigenous systems of crop cultivation were near perfect to begin with, and that humans have destroyed the functional systems only to be replaced with a huge barrage of poison and death and destruction for the earth, is too cataclysmic and defines all that modern science is built upon: a lack of connection with the earth and our own selves. We got short sighted and thought that somehow forcing the yields to be higher, by any method possible, is a good thing. We forgot to take the earth, the water, the millions of other beings into account, as if they don't exist, and only humans, one single species on the planet out of the billions, are the center of the Universe. *How did we ever hope that giving death and destruction to millions of other life forms could be good for us?*

Burning up the Atmosphere

It is sometimes difficult to imagine that one industry can be so damaging to the environment in so many ways, and yet it keeps growing at a remarkable rate, without any major policy intervention or changes in the way it operates. Discount the updates to meals given in canteens in some college and university or some company; most of the world is still conveniently unconcerned about the environmental impact of something that makes up a big part of their lives every day: their food.

When one enjoys a snack, and sees the winter colder than it should be, or the summer hotter than it should be, one does not normally think of the snack on their plate, because the linking happens through many infinitesimal parts. But there is a link alright, and it needs to be understood, so you can make a link between every action you take and hurting or harming your habitat and your own self. It is important to understand the *karmic* footprint of your actions as well as the carbon footprint of your actions.

The climate is altered, sometimes irreparably, with the growing amount of greenhouse gases in the atmosphere. These gases make the Earth warmer or colder than it should be, depending on where you are. It can cause natural calamities, if the glaciers and the ice caps melt at an unsustainable rate, and can cause both economic losses as well as loss of human life and animal life. Much of the biodiversity of the earth will also get destroyed as a part of these calamities.

This phenomenon was called "global warming," and has now been referred to as "climate change" by scientists. Whatever be the name, the underlying facts are that the growing accumulation of greenhouse gases in the Earth's atmosphere are ***changing the way we live.*** It is not just a problem that needs to be prevented for the future, it is a problem that is already here, and we are already suffering with it. The only reason we don't know that this is a problem is that the process of alteration of the climate involves thousands of steps, over several years, across geographical borders, and hence it is a daunting task to definitively say with authority that a particular forest fire was an outcome of climate change or a particular avalanche was an outcome of climate change. There is no clear methodology to draw the causal link between different incidents. Yet, if we sit back and look upon what is happening to the Earth, it is hard to imagine that the damage caused by us to the Earth's atmosphere is innocuous. It requires a great deal of unconsciousness to truly believe that we can keep hurting the Earth and all its creatures, and the Earth will not punish us back or not fight back to protect itself. *"Climate change" is, really, just another word for Nature's fury.*

Nature, the Earth, are not matter, they are living entities. They are replete with the same life energy and life force that keeps us all alive. They vibrate with the same divinity that we experience in our own selves in moments of calm and bliss. So, if we, as humans who are the most evolved of all creatures, do not live up to our consciousness and continuously harm that divinity in nature, there will be repercussions and those repercussions were called as "global warming" in the last decade and are called as "climate change" these days. The word may change a decade later, but the overarching principle remains the same.

These repercussions have an impact on many aspects of our lives, some measurable, and many immeasurable. The economic impact of climate change is not just to catalogue the economic losses, but rather, **a metric that attempts to capture the overall impact of the damage caused to the Earth**, that everyone can understand. Everyone understands the language of money. So, if we say that the Amazon forests of Brazil are burning at the rate of three football fields per minute (Lauren Frias, 2019), many may not consider it something worth bothering themselves with, since it is happening so far away, and they don't even know what the Amazon forests look like. But if we say that the impact of 2.5 Kelvin increase in temperature of the atmosphere of the Earth will effectively cause a person to feel like they have lost 1.3% of their income, you would probably find most people doing the maths to evaluate how much money they are going to lose. Money is a language everyone understands. So, it is worth understanding the numbers behind the losses, and paying some close attention to the same.

As per a report by United Nations and CRED in 2017 (*Economic Losses, Poverty & Disasters*, 2017), for the period between 1998 and 2017, the total figure for economic losses worldwide due to natural calamities stands at 2.9 trillion USD. Of this, the biggest losers are USA (945 billion$), China (492.2 billion$), Japan (376.3 billion$) and India (79.5 billion$). The number of lives lost in natural calamities is 1.3 billion, with another 4.4 billion severely injured. A big percentage of these disasters are attributed to climate change. The total loss due to climate-change related disasters is estimated at 2,245$.

> *"For disasters since 2000, georeferencing has found that in low-income countries, an average of 130 people died per million living in disaster-affected areas, compared to just 18 in high income countries. That means people exposed to natural hazards in the poorest nations were more than seven times more likely to die than equivalent populations in the richest nations." - UN report*

Agriculture is one of the major culprits in contributing to atmospheric Greenhouse Gas Emissions (GHGE), and the

Global greenhouse gas emissions from food production

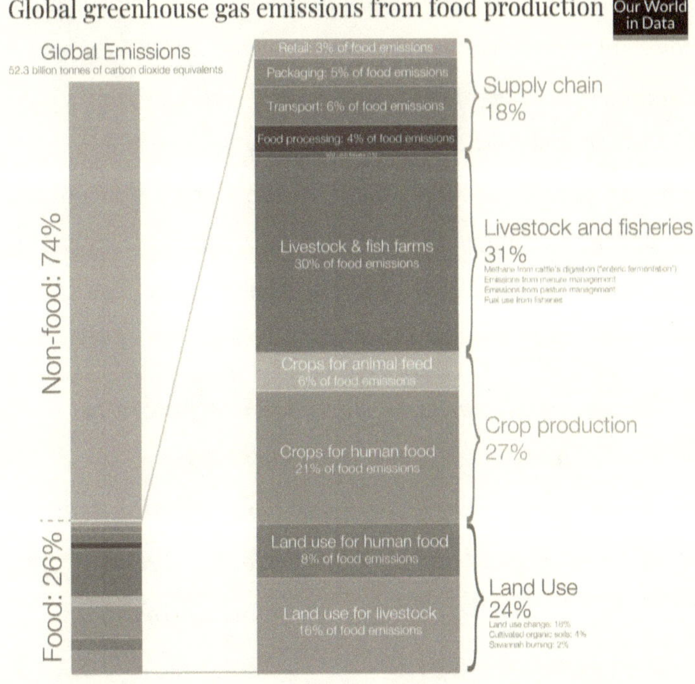

food system is an even bigger culprit, since it includes some of the processes in addition to those included in agricultural practices. **Food contributes to 26% of the world's GHG emissions.** The meat and dairy industry in general, and livestock farming in specific, are a major contributor to the world's GHGEs by themselves. The most common and important anthropogenic GHGEs are N_2O, CO_2 and CH_4 (Methane), and the meat and dairy industries emit all three. For a comparative measure, GHGEs are calculated as CO_2 equivalent or CO_2, but it can be a trifle misleading, since different gases have different times of "residence" in the atmosphere, and different capacity to warm up the atmosphere. Methane is approximately 28 times more powerful than CO_2 in warming up the atmosphere, on a hundred-year scale, and 80 times more powerful than CO_2 on a 20-year scale. Humans are squarely responsible for the growing percentage of methane in the Earth's atmosphere. Livestock contributes to 14.5% of global Methane emissions (Kumari et al., 2018) and is the biggest source of anthropogenic Methane emissions.

> *"Dairy buffalo and indigenous dairy cattle together contribute 60% of the total methane emission. The three high methane emitter states are Uttar Pradesh (14.9%), Rajasthan (9.1%) and Madhya Pradesh (8.5%)."—Spatial pattern of methane emissions from Indian livestock (Abha Chhabra et al., 2009)*

Nitrous Oxide is the other GHGE, and the livestock sector contributes to 32% of anthropogenic emissions of N_2O (Uwizeye et al., 2020). Nitrous Oxide has a long "residence time" in the atmosphere—150 years. It has a higher potential to trap heat in the atmosphere than CO_2; its radiative-forcing potential is 310 times that of CO_2. It also has another damaging effect on the atmosphere—it can get photolytically oxidized to Nitric Oxide, NO, and eat into the Ozone layer in the stratosphere, thus allowing more of ultraviolet radiation to the Earth, adding to the build-up of heat.

There have been multiple studies that assess the environmental impact of different diets in different countries.

These studies assess the impact a change of diet would have on the GHGEs and other related environmental factors like land, water, deforestation etc.

A study of Dutch diets (van de Kamp et al., 2018) found that the diet which includes lower meat had lowered the GHGEs by one third. Another study on the diets in the European Union (Westhoek et al., 2014) assessed the impact of lowering meat and dairy consumption on agriculture and emissions. They found that lowering livestock production lowered Nitrogen emissions by 40%, and GHGEs by 25-40%. Halving dairy and meat intake brought down the saturated fats consumption level to maximum recommended dietary guidelines, giving significant health benefits. It would also bolster the economy by making EU an exporter of cereals, as the increased demand for cereals (to maintain same calorific intake) will be outrun by decreased demand of livestock feed. It would also reduce the imports of soybean by 75%. The average land-use for food per EU citizen will be reduced from 0.23 to 0.17 hectares. A report that examines (Bryngelsson et al., 2016) how the EU can meet their 2050 climate target for reduction of emissions to bring down the projected 2°C increase in global temperature, indicates that the targets can be met, but will require a significant reduction—50%—in meat consumption in the EU.

Large reductions, by 50% or more, in ruminant meat (beef and mutton) consumption are, most likely, unavoidable if the EU targets are to be met (Bryngelsson et al., 2016).

Another study, done in India (R. F. Green et al., 2018), found that rice and meat-based diets had the highest negative impact on the environment, with the maximum GHGEs and higher green water footprint. Since a big percentage of India lives below poverty line, a big percentage of Indians currently do not consume nutrients per the dietary food guidelines and hence do not contribute to GHGEs or the water footprint much. This, combined with the country's cultural preference for vegetarianism is a strong factor in keeping our GHGEs due to agriculture low. But the impact of the dairy industry is still significant. Considering a preferential shift towards meaty diets in the country, with growing economic affluence, the problem of growing GHGEs in the coming decades is a real concern that needs to be addressed now, not 10 years later when the dietary patterns have already changed for the worse.

The biggest challenge with understanding the impact of GHGEs to the environment and our everyday lives is that it is not something you can see, smell, hear, eat or touch. The emissions cannot be perceived with our senses. In a world which is continuously overwhelmed and overloaded with sensory stimulation, it is very easy to ignore the impact of emissions associated with your food on the environment and your own self. It is hard enough for people to make sense of what they do see, hear, taste, touch and smell. To seriously reckon the impact of something they do not understand or perceive, is a Herculean task for most people. This is why it is very easy to deny the impact *altogether*. It is very easy and convenient to say that it has no impact, and also, to misrepresent the impact—both in terms of overestimating it and underestimating it. Political will can choose to push the impact one way or the other, without a simple, verifiable way to know that it is being misrepresented. This is part of the reason why climate change is not taken seriously by people, and even though intuitively it makes every sense, in spite of there being empirical research to prove its economic impact and cost to human lives, people are reluctant to change the habits and lifestyles to allow for climate change reformist plans.

Even more important, but overlooked, is the shift in food *culture* required for achieving the goals of lower GHGEs. While policies can incentivize and de-incentivize certain behavioural patterns, a strong awakening and awareness in the masses on what they are eating and where their food fits in the catastrophes the world is facing is important to implement the shifts in dietary patterns required to go carbon neutral.

Brazil's Dwindling Rainforests and the Hamburger Connection

Brazil is world's third largest consumer (Rob Cook, 2021) **of beef.** It consumes 13% of all beef produced globally. It is also the highest beef consumer per capita, alongside the USA. Brazil is also the world's largest exporter of beef, alongside India.

Beef in Brazil comes primarily from cows, many of which are Zebu cows imported from India. These cows require pastures for grazing, and cow feed for consumption. To meet these requirements, land needs to be cleared up for creating "pastures" and fields.

Brazil ran out of its share of pastoral land many years ago. The answer to the problem? **Forests of Amazon.**

The forests of Amazon are rain forests: meaning they create their own rain, to a great extent, in layman terms. These forests are a unique ecosystem, where the thick vegetation and trees are part responsible for the rainfall they receive, due to evapotranspiration. Simply put, no forest = no rain. The virtuous cycle of rain and flourishing forests will end if there were no forests left. The land will become parched, and it will be impossible to create a forest out of that land again.

Deforestation in the Amazonia (Sarah Holder, 2019) has been going on for several decades. Brazil has been seeing forest fires year in and year out, with the number and intensity of fires setting new records in 2019.

Deforestation is a problem that affects multiple generations, for the simple reason that once a part of the forest is burnt, it does not grow back. **So the yearly forest fires are a compounded problem.** Even if, perceptually speaking, the "rate" of the fire in a subsequent year is less, it only lessens the spread of the problem, does not eliminate it, and does not undo the problem already created in the previous years. Every year's deforestation is added on top of the deforestation that has already happened. It leaves a charred landscape behind, the perfect picture of devastation, in place of lush green vegetation and teeming wildlife.

The worst part is that most of these **forest fires are manmade**: they are started by humans, for multiple reasons, mostly illegal.

Causes of Forest Fires: "The Hamburger Connection"

The beef industry is squarely to blame (SARAH GIBBENS, 2019) for the unabated fires in the Amazon forests of Brazil.

Though the world woke up to this menace only recently, the speedily booming beef industry in Brazil has translated to thinner and thinner forest cover over the last few decades. Much of the food grown, as part of agribusiness, is also meant to feed cows, or exported to countries like China, to feed their livestock. So, indirectly, the agribusiness is also flourishing—and eating into the Amazon rain forests—due to the beef industry.

The beef industry in Brazil saw an upward rise in the late 1990's and early 2000's. This should have rung alarm bells, but instead was allowed to grow, as it contributed monetarily to the country's economy, with mounting beef exports, ignoring the destruction of the forests, which is the painful cost which came with the industrial scale of expansion of beef industry.

According to the Yale School of Forestry and Environmental Studies,

> *"Approximately 450,000 square kilometers of deforested Amazon in Brazil are now in cattle pasture."*

In the pastureland cleared up from deforestation, pastoral land is 10 times the amount of land used for growing grains.

In Brazil, pastureland outweighs planted cropland by about 5 times.

Hypothetically speaking, if the world were to turn vegan or vegetarian and stop eating beef altogether, the global demand for beef would cascade down. This would mean that the land currently available for agriculture would suffice to grow the food required by human beings, and there would be no further need to burn down the forest–neither for pastoral land, nor for agribusiness.

Fallout of Deforestation: Hello, Climate Change

Since the 1970's, **Brazil has lost nearly 800,000 km² of forest cover.** This is an area bigger than the state of Texas. The Amazon forests are home to 400 billion trees, and release one fifth of the globe's oxygen. Every time a chunk of the forest is burnt, the oxygen supply to the planet is cut off. The Amazon forests store approximately 90 billion metric tonnes of Carbon. Burning the forests releases toxic fumes, adding to the planet's GHG emissions by releasing this additional carbon currently stored in the forests.

With the forests gone, the goal of containing global warming to 2°Celsius looks ambitious and unrealistic. This is sending chills down the spines of climate scientists, who are quite sure that exceeding this goal will have catastrophic effects globally. Rise of temperatures and extremes of climates is only one of the effects.

The ice caps are melting, causing the sea levels to rise globally. This is loss of habitable land along the coast lines. Wildlife is getting destroyed as we speak. Animals are dying and homeless. The beef production process itself uses up natural resources like fresh water and fossil fuels, adding further to the global carbon footprint. Fumes from the forest fires are choking citizens in Brazilian cities, possibly causing respiratory disorders and diseases, which will be uncovered a few years later.

So much destruction, death, and disease, unleashed on the planet simply because humans cannot drop their irrational infatuation with beef.

Environmental Footprint of your Boots

Leather is an industry which is poised comfortably between the meat and dairy industries, and hence, easily escapes the blame for animal cruelty, damaging the environment, and other such evils which are a by-product of the shoes, bags and wallets made of dead animals' skins. The blame for many such evils is shifted on to the meat and dairy industries, although the leather industry causes a huge amount of damage too, and not just to the environment. It is very easy, convenient and "normal" to forget about what the animals have to face for that bag or wallet, and what the environment looks like before and after we are done with the tanning.

It is a grand myth that only dead animals' skins are used for leather. It is a myth everyone likes to believe because it is easy to believe it, because believing it makes us feel that it is ethical, and it is okay to do so. The other myth circulated by the leather industry is that it is not damaging to the environment, especially water. Since it is a thriving industry which has not come under the scanner as much, both these myths are common arguments, along with the economic profits from the industry, to allow the existence of the industry as-is.

The truth is that very often the step of the process which involves skinning an animal is physically separated from the process where the hides are tanned to convert it to leather. Physical separation of the two parts of the process does not necessarily mean that the two are independent of each other. Animals are slaughtered in slaughterhouses, where they are also skinned. These hides are then sent to tanneries, which are often along the rivers, for tanning and conversion to leather. Tanneries buy hides from slaughterhouses. Slaughterhouses and farms raise animals in large numbers for the purpose of meat and leather both, along with dairy, where cows and buffaloes are slaughtered.

In India, since cow slaughter is banned in many states, cows are transported to states like Kerala and Tamil Nadu in inhuman conditions, deprived of food and water. Some collapse and die on the way. Others are mutilated and tortured with chilies in their eyes so they can't escape. As many as 50 cows are often packed in one truck (the number of allowed cows is six), where they have no room to breathe. The conditions are extremely unhygienic, needless to say. So it is not just the ultimate slaughter which is cruel to animals, but their whole life is a punishment to them. In some countries, even this does not sufficiently describe the reality of leather, since many animals are *boiled alive* for their skins, and they are flayed afterwards, when they are still alive and conscious.

Leather by itself does not have much color, only texture. Its texture is enhanced, and colors added to it by chemically processing it with tannins. There are multiple processes for tanning, but they all include dissolving chemicals, most of which have heavy metals like Chromium, in water as a solvent and stirring the hides to allow the chemicals to alter the dead skin cells to change their color and enhance the skin texture. A lot of the process, though, involves manual work—like plucking out hair from the skin by hand. It is unfortunate that human beings have become desensitized enough to not consider this type of work as unfit for physical or mental health of anyone, and cruel to animals. When humans work in these conditions, where cruelty and violence are a way of life, how can we possibly hope to have a society where violence and cruelty to each other is an aberration?

It is estimated that India has more than 2000 tanneries, and produces more than 2 million square feet of leather annually (Larry C. Price & Debbie M. Price, 2017), contributing to 12.9% of the world's leather supply (as of 2020) (*Leather Industry: Indian Leather Exports & Manufacturers in India | IBEF*, 2021). India's leather exports added up to approximately 5.07 billion USD (as of 2019-2020). Main leather centers in India are Tamil Nadu, West Bengal and Uttar Pradesh, combined with other zones like Dharavi in Mumbai. India is the second largest exporter of leather garments in the world, owing to its huge cattle population. This is no matter of pride for us, in a country where the cow is considered sacred by the majority. That our economy needs to grow and prosper from cruelty to the cow is not a matter of pride; it is paradoxical to everything Hindus consider sacred.

Water from tanneries flows into rivers, water bodies and other water supply channels. This toxic water waste from tanneries contains heavy metals which are carcinogenic. Although many tanneries claim to recycle their water waste, many do not do so, or do not recycle all of their waste water. To show compliance with laws, some percentage of the water is recycled, while the rest is dumped into the rivers as-is.

In 2013, a study reported that Indian tanneries in Kanpur were pumping out 300 million liters (PETE MCBRIDE, 2014) of contaminated water into the Ganga river per day, but the water treatment facility could only handle 170 million liters of water per day. So, a huge percentage of water dumped into the Ganga—which is the source of water for all of North India—is contaminated with heavy metals. A water test on water samples collected along the Ganga found 21 heavy metals in the water, with a high percentage of Chromium. Chromium is the chief metal used in tannins. The leather industry is directly responsible for polluting the main rivers of India, but this toxicity is completely overlooked and undermined in front of the economic profits. It is estimated that over 55,000 hectares of land have been contaminated (Dixit et al., 2015) due to toxic water from tanneries, affecting around 5 million people, who do not have any feasible options for drinking water. In a country which already has a problem of safe drinking water, these toxic wastes worsen the crisis and aggravate the poverty situation in villages and small towns. It is now another added challenge for someone living below poverty line to obtain clean drinking water.

We do not even have an intelligent estimate of the economic losses, and the cost to human life, from this toxic water. But, we know for a fact that pollution is the leading cause of global premature deaths, with one in seven of these deaths due to pollution of water, air and soil. All because we do not care about cows getting slaughtered, skinned and tortured for that strap of leather. The cruelty meted out to other creatures finds a way to circle back to our own selves. We have just become very lousy in tracing the entire circle.

The visual reality of tanneries is so unsavoury, that it comes as little surprise that no one visits them, or even knows the working conditions in the tanneries or what they contribute to the environment. Skins of dead animals piled up everywhere. Floors blue with tannins. Blood oozing from hides. Not a spot of clean floor to walk on, or clean air to breathe. Unused hides rotting in piles of trash outside tanneries. Dirty water pouring into rivers by the gallon. And an animal who had to lose its life so someone could carry a fashionable handbag.

There are numerous alternatives to leather today, including vegan leather and synthetic or faux leathers. In India, unsurprisingly, approximately 90% of the shoe industry relies on synthetic leathers. Due to religious and economic reasons, many Indians do not buy leather. Even today, leather is not allowed in temples or any religious procession or rituals. The proclivity for leather is a modern phenomenon, and does not have origins in Indian or Hindu culture, as we shall see later.

Symbiotic relationship between cow and humans

The blows we deal out to animals hurt us back via the damage we cause to our environment, and to our own bodies, ruining our health, as we shall see a little later in the book. But is there a way to live with animals by which we nurture animals, rather than torture them? Most assuredly, yes. Symbiosis is the way of nature to exist. Deep in the forests, we see plants, organisms, animals, all living symbiotically. They do not harm each other. They co-exist in a mutually enriching way. Ferns grow on trees. Tree is not hurt from that. Orphan animal cubs are fed by species of other animals. These are not aberrations in nature. This is the way of life which exists everywhere, in places where humans have not yet left their footprints of insatiable greed and exploitation of nature's resources, leading to destruction.

As per Hindu culture, what you empower, drives you. If you empower kindness towards other, it will empower you back.

The famous Hindu adage *"Dharmo Rakshati Rakshitah"* means that Dharma is that, which when protected, protects you. As such, the ancient Hindu society lived with animals in a symbiotic relationship, where we nurtured animals, especially cattle, and they nurtured us back, leading to prosperity and growth for all. True prosperity cannot be built on the tears of the blameless. That can be money, but not prosperity—it will have no stability. An economy built on simply amassing money, currency, but which is based in violence, will not be stable.

There are more than a few lessons from India's indigenous people, their Hindu culture, and how that culture has evolved technologically to lead the way towards more ecologically, and economically savvy solutions. Technology and culture do not need to be at odds with each other. In fact, some of the best innovations in technology improve or improvise upon existing indigenous methods and make them accessible to more people in more efficient ways.

So, it is important to take a long, hard look at what we are using technology *for,* and where it is leading us. A lot of the modern systems in use were an outcome of wars, colonization and destruction of indigenous traditions and methods of existence—which were, by default, methods of coexisting peacefully with all of life and nature. Colonial powers, by-products of chemical warfare and the insatiable greed of humans led us to unsustainable systems, which destroy animals, destroy nature, destroy our habitat, destroy our health, and eventually destroy everything life is worth living for.

So, we need to revisit what we have labelled as "primitive" or "backward" and what we have labelled as "modern" and "progressive." We need a thorough re-evaluation of every method, without the jaundiced eye of "this is the traditional method, hence unscientific" and "this was created in a laboratory, hence this is scientific." The purpose of science is simply to study life, and suggest solutions based on that study. Science is open architecture—it can be updated, and it should be updated. We need to acknowledge and own up our failings. We need a systematic revival and implementation of all methods—modern or traditional—that are sustainable, and have zero cost to nature, ecosystems, environment, and animals. The cost human beings pay out of their pockets is not the only cost to be considered. The cost that others pay, sometimes with their lives, is also a cost. We have simply deleted them from our framework of reference. We need a new reference frame. ***We need to consider the karmic footprint of our actions, not just the carbon footprint of our establishments.***

Brew Your Own Cooking Gas

Manure waste management has always been a big problem for cow shelters and dairy farms, both from hygiene, as well as from emissions point of view. Indians knew this early on, since the cow was at the center of our lives. Every household either had a cow or knew a household that had a cow, till about a hundred years ago. So, we needed a solution for managing the waste early on. So far, cow dung was mainly used for making dried cow dung cakes, used as fuel in *"choolhas"* and fresh manure was used as a disinfecting paint on walls, due to its anti-microbial properties. So, we were already aware of the potential of manure as a fuel since time immemorial. But a few scientific minds took it one step further and decided to tap into the Methane emissions from the manure and put it to good use: as cooking gas and an alternative to fossil fuels.

Although the concept of anaerobic digestion was under research in most of Europe in the 19th century, the credit for developing the first anaerobic digester goes to India. Indian scientists built a functioning biogas digester which converted human waste to gas in 1897. Indian scientists also built the first ever biogas plant in 1937. By the 1940s, households in Indian villages already had "Gobar Gas" or biogas units installed, and utilized the gas for cooking purposes, and the leftover sludge as an organic fertilizer on farms. China took a leaf out of India's book, and in a few decades, outpaced India in installing the number of biogas units in the country. The Chinese used all types of waste in their digesters, and hence grew at a faster pace. This is one of the ways in which China reduced its energy costs while also growing economically. China has the biggest biogas program in the world, with more than 26.55 million biogas units in the country (as of 2007).

The apparatus and its installation is simple enough, and is cost effective in the long run. In India, the apparatus costs approximately INR 20,000. Cooking gas costs approximately INR 1000 per cylinder. So in two years, the installation will be paying for itself. Moreover, the anaerobically digested sludge or digestate yields organic biofertilizer, saving costs of fertilizers. Production of inorganic fertilizers has a high cost, both economically, and in terms of the amount of fossil fuels consumed in the process. By using home-made organic fertilizer, the financial costs as well as environmental costs of fertilizers can be reduced, or brought down to zero, making the farms completely sustainable.

Unlike other biofuels, biogas does not require anything other than already plentifully existing dung, wastes and night soil. Other biofuels require special crops to be grown, like soy and corn, which take up huge pastures which could have been forests. In Brazil, one of the reasons for destruction of the forests of Amazonia is the requirement for pastures to grow corn and soy, so as to export the crops for manufacture of biofuels. Though biofuels are an alternate energy source, they do have a high cost to the environment as well.

Since biogas is essentially a decentralized fuel generation system, it also hedges many risks and costs associated with a central supply: costs of transportation, changes in pricing, short supply and unavailability etc.

Another incentive for using biogas in villages is the lack of suitable alternatives for cooking: villagers use straw, cow dung cakes, twigs, newspaper, or just about anything that is combustible! Villagers were using open flame stoves, with combustible items that could potentially cause health risks before biogas became popular in villages. Usage of kerosene oil stoves, or paper, dried leaves as fuel for cooking gives out fumes which when inhaled for prolonged periods of time can cause diseases of the lungs. Coal is the other fuel used, but being a fossil fuel, it is again at a high cost to the environment. Open flame stoves were the leading cause of indoor air pollution in India as per recent studies. Many villagers live in small houses and huts, where it is not even possible for them to get a cooking gas line connection and buying a gas cylinder means transporting it over long distances. Biogas plant installation in your backyard solves this problem.

Since biogas is a fuel, it paves the way for economically efficient production of electricity. Many states in India still do not meet their power requirements. States like Uttar Pradesh, Uttarakhand, even Karnataka, still have frequent power cuts, and many villages, though now electrified, do not receive the requisite amount of electricity. Illegally directing wirelines to power up houses is common in slums and shanties. When there are frequent power cuts, people use diesel powered generators to keep their establishments running. This has a colossal environmental cost. It causes pollution, and increases our fossil fuel demand. People will power up their homes and businesses one way or another, with what is available. And what is available is neither sufficient, nor viable.

India needs more electricity.

India has taken huge strides in moving towards renewable energy sources, but still has a lot of untapped potential in the form of biogas. Were India to realize its full potential of converting cow dung and other wastes to biogas and biofertilizers, and then to electricity, one of the biggest challenges of both poverty, as well as climate change, will be addressed in one brilliant stroke.

India is home to the world's largest livestock population—approximately 512 million (as of 2017), with approximately 303 million cattle. Assuming that one cow produces 10 kg of dung every day, that is more than 3 billion kg of cow dung per day, with additional dung from other livestock, available as a ready resource to brew biogas, biofertilizers and electricity. As per research, 1 kg of cow dung, mixed with equal quantity of water, and left for retention for 60 days, yields 35-40 liters of biogas. Calculations for different states in India, for the year 2017, yielded the final figure as 157,870 million m3 per annum biogas production capacity for the whole country. This amounts to energy of 5,146,576 million MJ per annum. Based on calculations (Kaur et al., 2017) for electricity production, this quantity of energy has the capacity to produce 477 TWhr of electricity per annum, which is no small figure.

We must keep in mind that these calculations only take into account the power generated with animal manure. In an anaerobic digester, on the other hand, crop stubble, agricultural wastes, night soil, industrial wastes and dried leaves etc. can all be added along with animal manure. So the real potential is going to be much higher than this figure. Moreover, we have not taken into account the amount of fuel and electricity saved by using organic biofertilizer instead of inorganic fertilizers which guzzle huge quantities of water and fossil fuels, give out chemical wastes, and are bad for health as well. On the other hand, the manure, which would otherwise have given out GHGEs, is now recycled into biogas and electricity, reducing the GHG load on the environment due to manure, lowering our contribution to increasing global temperatures. So, to perform a real cost-benefit analysis of using biogas, all of these factors need to be considered. Biogas is more than just an alternative fuel. It can help solve our clean energy crisis, lead to better agricultural practices, cleaner environment, lower emissions, healthier alternatives for people, and reduce our costs and dependency on fertilizer imports.

Pull Back the Carbon et al

Carbon sequestration is a complicated word, but gaining increasing popularity of late, for what it means: pulling back the carbon from the atmosphere, and binding it into the soil or some other carbon sink, in a semi-permanent or permanent way. By "carbon", we really mean the carbon emissions here, which are the cause of greenhouse gas effect, and climate change.

Of the technologies that exist today to pull back the carbon, one lies in our own backyards: manure. The technical term for it is Farmyard Manure (FYM).

Soil is considered to be the best, most technically feasible option for binding back the carbon emissions in the atmosphere, as Soil Organic Carbon (SOC). But, due to deteriorating, environmentally insensitive agricultural practices, the available potential of soil to sequester carbon has been declining. The causes and solutions for this need to be urgently looked into. While a segment of the scientific community racks its brains on new technologies to sequester carbon from the atmosphere, we already have a solution available. We just need to understand how to utilize that potential, and alter agricultural practices to improve the situation. There is nothing wrong with coming up with new technologies, but it is a folly to overlook and gloss over an already existing solution that can be applied at a vast scale all over the world.

The process of creation of biogas yields biofertilizer as a byproduct, which helps farmers in low budget organic farming. But, apart from being low budget and environmentally efficient, it has an additional advantage of having the capacity to sequester carbon from the atmosphere (Tsachidou et al., 2021) when used as a fertilizer.

Both, farmyard manure, and biofertilizers, have the capacity to sequester carbon. The nitty gritty details of the most effective crop rotation cycles for this objective to be achieved vary greatly, from one region to another, based on the type of soil, water table, climatic conditions, terrain, type of crops, and available resources. Numerous studies have been performed to assess the efficacy of carbon sequestration with manure and biofertilizer in different scenarios, and as per this review of 74 such studies (Andreas Gattinger et al., 2012), it was found that biofertilizer and manure bind a lot more carbon into the soil than inorganic NPK fertilizers. The dataset for the study comprised all climatic zones. The data clearly showed that organic management systems increased SOC.

Many people know about the potential of cow dung to sequester carbon into the soil. But what is often overlooked is its capacity for nitrogen fixation from the atmosphere into the soil, improving the fertility of the soil. When a mixture of cow dung and soil is left exposed to the atmosphere, it undergoes oxidation, and in the process, binds atmospheric nitrogen into the soil, improving the nitrogen content of the soil. These findings were first known in the 20th century. This is not a new phenomenon. In 1936, a note on the findings of a field study (DHAR & MUKERJI, 1936) reported increase of nitrogen percentage from 0.0905% in July to 0.14% in November in a mixture of 100 gm freshly collected cow dung and 500gm soil. Other field reports demonstrated that for grasslands, the nitrogen content of soil increased from 0.152% in 1856 to 0.338% in 1912, on application of farmyard manure. Similarly, a land completely covered (Dhar, 1943) with vegetation for 24 years, showed a marked increase of soil nitrogen content from 0.108% to 0.145% total nitrogen. The addition of other compounds like molasses, carbohydrates, glycerol, dextrin, cellulosic compounds like paper, hay, fats like butter, ghee, salts of palmitic, oleic, stearic, citric, tartaric, malic, oxalic, acetic acids etc., when mixed with soil or chemical surfaces like the oxides of zinc, aluminium, iron, manganese, nickel, cobalt and copper, have the capacity to fix nitrogen under both aerobic and anaerobic conditions in the soil. Carbonaceous organic matter helps in binding nitrogen to the soil.

Thus, use of farmyard manure and organic fertilizers have the potential to bind atmospheric nitrogen emissions as well, which contribute to the Greenhouse Gas Effect. They add nutrition value to the soil, which are sustained over long periods of time.

There is one more item in the list of wonders of cow dung, as far as saving the environment goes. Cow dung is a perfect adsorbent to sequester heavy metals, glyphosate and aminomethylphosphonic acid (AMPA) from the soil and water. Adsorption is a process by which a substance (adsorbate) is transferred from the liquid state to the surface of a solid (adsorbent) and becomes bound there by chemical or physical attraction.

Glyphosate is a herbicide used extensively by farmers. Its usage is a growing environmental concern, since it percolates into the ground water and can contaminate the soil and water. It can cause leaching and ground water contamination, which, depending on the mobility of the water, can spread to a large area beyond just the farms. Its effects on aquatic animals are severe: it is a growth inhibitor and increases their mortality rate. Both glyphosate and its degradation product AMPA are equally toxic, and high concentrations of both have been found in reservoirs, ground water runoffs and samples from other water sources in USA and Brazil. There is no reason to believe that this would not be the case in other countries where glyphosate is freely used. Thus, removing glyphosate and AMPA are of huge environmental significance.

Conventional methods of water filtration are firstly expensive, and secondly, almost ineffective in removing pollutants that are water soluble. Activated carbon remains the most widely used method for filtering water of soluble impurities, but it is an expensive method, which is difficult to scale and loses its efficacy after some time. Cow dung wins on both scores. It is readily available at low costs, and is effective in adsorbing both the pollutants for extended periods of time. Here, "cow dung" refers to the excreta of cows, calves, bulls and heifers, not just the cow. A study (Garba et al., 2019) on the adsorption efficacy of cow dung demonstrated it to be a viable bioadsorbent for both the pollutants.

Cow dung ash, also called *"Bhasma"* by Hindus, is, on the other hand, an effective adsorbent for heavy metals. Heavy metals are toxic even in small quantities, and can find their way into food systems through polluted water and soil. Industrial waste discharge is the top factor responsible for the presence of heavy metals in soil and water. Cow dung ash is an ecofriendly and cost-effective agent to help adsorb the toxic compounds out of water. Cow dung ash contains (Ojedokun & Bello, 2016) calcium oxide, magnesium oxide, calcium sulphate, aluminium oxide, iron oxide and a high percentage of silica. The presence of high concentration of silica gives it a high affinity for metal ions. Unlike other adsorbents, cow dung does not give out a foul odor during the process. This process was analyzed in a study (Ojedokun & Bello, 2016), and cow dung ash was considered to be a clean, cheap and highly effective adsorbent for removing heavy metal from aqueous solutions. This is technology that requires more research and development, and has not yet been implemented at a large scale. When we consider the loss of life due to toxins in food systems, and the loss of arable land due to ground water pollution, utilizing an existing resource for "cleaning up our act" seems extremely economically viable.

Cow dung has numerous uses, apart from those already listed. It can be made into incense that works as a mosquito repellent. It is common to see it used in this form in Indian villages. It can also be blended with mud to prepare bricks for climatically responsive construction. So the waste generated from cows need not go waste. They can effectively make a country go carbon neutral, or even carbon negative. In a research paper (Budzianowski, 2011) that analyses the usage of biogas and electricity generation in Poland, the author examines how this gamut of technologies centered on cow dung can be used to be carbon negative. The author evaluates biogas as a carbon neutral electricity source, and considers the three routes—biogas to biomethane, biogas to electricity and biogas to CHP—as ways of realizing a carbon negative country. His analysis is reflective of the possibilities of building an economy around environmentally conscious and economically viable choices.

This is not to suggest that we can make up for the loss of forest cover by implementing organic farming practices in the pastures thus cleared, but to move away from inorganic fertilizers, and implement environmentally conscious farming systems as far as possible. Implementing only a part solution cannot solve the complex, multi-tiered problem of damage to the environment due to the cruel and unsustainable meat, dairy and leather industries. Only when the fundamental ideas change, and there is a tangible shift in the way we seek solutions, can we stop damaging the environment, and then move ahead towards fixing it.

There are many meat activist groups that suggest that there is no "economic viability" of cows that are not lactating anymore, and oxen and male calves who will never yield milk. Thus, they should be killed and consumed as meat. The meat lobbyists present this argument to justify the killing of livestock. It is a different matter that the breeding of animals for meat is not limited to just male calves or non-lactating cows, but rather, there is an orchestrated effort to force cattle to reproduce as fast and as much as possible, so as to have high yields of dairy and meat. But, the logic used to justify killing uses the twisted logic of "economics". The lobbyists present animal killing as a cost effective "solution" since killing, as per them, means they can make money from the meat, and they do not have to spend money on feeding the cattle for the rest of their lives. It is an approach fueled with greed, insensitivity and self-gratifying tendencies, which has little bearing in economics, and has no concern for the environment whatsoever. It is not a holistic approach.

As has already been discussed in most of this section on the environment and the meat, dairy and leather industry, the damage meted out to the environment and cruelty meted out to the animals comes back to bite us in numerous ways, through loss of topsoil, natural calamities, loss of water and droughts, shortage of food in some parts of the world, and as we will see in the next few chapters, loss of nutrition in food and serious damage to our health. So, reducing forced reproduction of cows through artificial insemination is what is needed urgently. We need to stop forcing animals to increase in a disbalanced, disproportionate manner, and stop killing the animals that already exist on the planet. Next, we need to make sure that all involved understand the downside of killing livestock and not gloat over short-term profits. A much more serious analysis and research is required in this domain, and the focus needs to shift there. As we saw in this chapter, during the course of its life, a cow or bull can provide us with cow dung for free, which can help solve the clean energy equation, provide lost cost fertilizer and also help solve the Carbon Capture and Storage (CCS) problem. When the waste of a cow can do so much for us, why would anyone want to kill it?

The Pandemic of Pandemics

The biggest pandemic on this planet is one that is spreading right under our noses, and has been doing so for the last fifty years or so: human beings' insatiably hedonistic lifestyles which destroy everything, including their own selves. An exploitative lifestyle is always going to be unsustainable, in every aspect of life. If we did not understand that even after being in the throes of the COVID-19 pandemic, maybe we should not be surprised about why it is not settling down. Nature is trying to teach us something that we are not learning.

Many of us saw the alarm bells ringing when we saw the extreme cruelty meted out to animals in every possible way. We knew that it could never lead to anything good. There was a storm coming. And the downside of any public health emergency is that nobody knows what to do, and political interests take precedence everywhere. If human beings really want to stay healthy and safe, they must start making changes in their own everyday choices, rather than depend on the government to take intelligent decisions for them. If you know what is the right thing to do, don't wait for someone else to do it for you or impose it on you. Take the first step.

More than 17 million minks were culled (Ollie Davidson, 2020) since November 2020 because they developed five new strains of the Corona virus, which were even more virulent and resistant to vaccines and antibodies. Yet, we still somehow believe that animal agriculture has no connection with pandemics. If sufficient research does not exist on the subject, that is an even bigger cause for concern: ***why are we not investigating something this important to human life?*** If the purpose of science is to understand all of life and give suggestions on how to improve the quality of life, why does this not get added to the list of to-dos?

When animals are caged in massive numbers in confined spaces, the hygiene levels can drop very quickly, making way for an environment that would cause quick spread of any pathogen. Since the animals live in fear, anxiety and stress, it is very natural for them to have very poor immune responses, and are, therefore, that much more likely to get pathogens. Moreover, as in the case of minks, there is very little genetic diversity in the animals, and that makes them of even poorer health and causes rapid spread of the virus. Though the case of minks was highlighted in the news, such cases of culling in animal agriculture keep cropping up, even though they never make the headlines.

As per one study (Jones et al., 2008), of the 335 Emerging Infectious Diseases (EID) events from 1940 to 2004, a big proportion—60.3%—are zoonoses, and of these 71.8% originated in wildlife. The results are observed to be significantly correlated with change in socio-economic, environmental and ecological patterns of human beings. There is a clear link between deforestation and virus emergence. With increased conversion of forest lands (Faust et al., 2018) into pastures for growing livestock feeds, mining, logging, building of roads, livestock and crop monocultures, there is disturbance and fragmentation in the natural habitat of wild animals, and a simultaneous increase in the perimeter of their contact with humans and livestock. The human and wildlife boundaries cross way too often, and the probability of pathogen spillover is high. Moreover, with livestock trapped in concentration camp like spaces, the contact between animals in animal farms is very high, and hence, even if one animal gets infected, the rest of the animal population on the farm can get infected in no time. In pandemics like SARS, Nipah, Ebola, and COVID, the host animals are bats, which live in the wild. In other pandemics like H1N1 and Avian flu, the virus spreads from livestock like pigs and chicken to humans.

Wildlife trades (Dobson et al., 2020) are the other major culprit in emergence of zoonotic viruses and other pathogens. Wild animals are captured in cages and transported across continents as "exotic pets". China is one such exporter, with a $ 20 billion industry, and USA is one of the biggest importers of wildlife. This is an immense risk, one which can easily multiply the spread of a virus manifold, very quickly, and across a huge geographical region. Livestock are transported across continents as well, in confined conditions. Due to the repeated emergence of different strains of swine flu and avian flu, a lot of livestock animals that are transported across continents are culled, as a public health concern. And yet, we do not stop to think about why we need to cull animals again and again and again and why we don't do away with situations that cause the virus in the first place.

One study estimates (Dobson et al., 2020) that proactive measures taken to reduce risks of spread from wildlife trade, animal agriculture and deforestation will cost far lesser than the cost of the actual pandemic, and help in supporting the environment, wildlife and biodiversity. They estimate that the cost of prevention of the next pandemic will be approximately 22-31.2 billion \$, whereas the cost of COVID-19 is expected to be 8.1-15.8 trillion \$. This factors in the benefits from carbon sequestration from the preventive measures, but there will also be numerous other benefits, outlined earlier in the book, which either cannot be estimated fairly, or may not necessarily have a monetary benefit, but have immense ecological benefits.

The biggest cost of pandemics is not just the economic cost due to the loss of human life. Even though we attach a "cost" to each life lost, in terms of monetary value, just to arrive at an estimate, economists know that this is by no means a fair measure. No one can measure the value of a human being in dollars. The biggest cost of the pandemic is the immense suffering caused to humanity, the innocent lives lost, the hopes and dreams of so many people crushed in a sleight of hand. So many millions others left to deal with the pain, loss and other struggles which are left in the wake of casualties and other challenges that a pandemic proposes.

With so much suffering as the aftermath, is that steak or that bacon really worth it?

What you eat is eating you

We eat food to stay healthy, nourished, energized, and ready to gear up and take on any challenges the world may throw our way. But what if what we eat itself is the challenge thrown our way? What if the shield is the sword sheering our worlds, without us even realizing it?

Meats make up a big part of our diets today, as illustrated in earlier chapters. Environmental concerns apart, is that, possibly a good thing for human beings? Is consumption of so much meat required for humans to survive? It is worthwhile to stop and ponder upon this question and take a long, hard look at what the numbers actually say.

As of 2009 (Ranganathan et al., 2016), on average, more than 90% people all over the world consumed more protein than the quantity as per the dietary recommendations. The average consumption was 68 gms/ day, which is at least 1/3rd more than the recommended quantity of protein. As per the recommended daily allowance (RDA) (Harvard Medical School, 2020), 0.8 grams per kilogram of body weight is sufficient for a healthy life.

For a 140-pound person, that comes to 51 grams of protein each day.

Figure ES-1 | Protein Consumption Exceeds Average Estimated Daily Requirements in All the World's Regions, and Is Highest in Developed Countries
g/capita/day, 2009

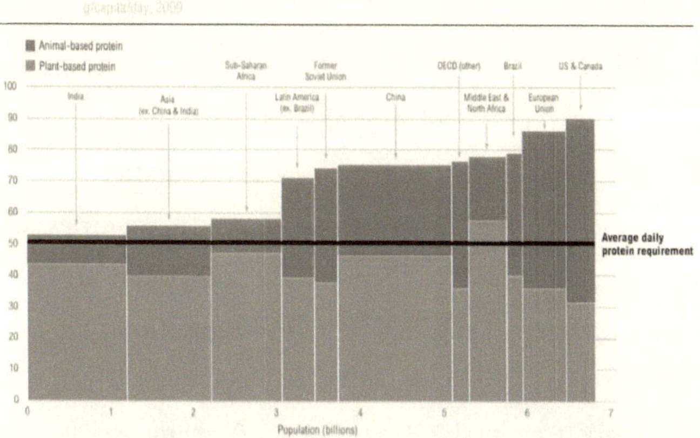

Source: GlobAgri model with source data from FAO (2016) and FAO (2011a). Width of bars is proportional to each region's population. Average daily protein requirement of 50 g/day is based on an average adult body weight of 62 kg (Walpole et al. 2012) and recommended protein intake of 0.8 g/kg body weight/day (Paul 1989). Individuals' energy requirements vary depending on age, gender, height, weight, pregnancy/lactation, and level of physical activity.

We are consuming more protein than required, in short, as seen from a plot of the data of protein consumption all over the world. A big part of this excess protein consumption is derived from animal proteins, namely, meats. For humans to reach their protein consumption to match dietary recommendations, they need only to increase their plant-based protein intake.

Does this level of consumption of protein have consequences, specifically, for health? The experts say, yes.

A study which (Delimaris, 2013) included analysis of 32 studies on the subject, identified high protein consumption to be associated with heightened risk of disorders of bone and calcium homeostasis, disorders of renal function, cancer, disorders of liver function, and precipitated progression of coronary artery disease. There is no good news as far as excessive protein consumption is concerned, even though the meat industry would have you believe otherwise.

In February 2019, the Lancet Commission sent recommendations (Willett et al., 2019) for alterations to the Dietary Guidelines for Americans, drafted by 19 commissioners and 18 co-authors from 16 countries, from multiple disciplines like agriculture, health, political sciences and environmental sustainability. These guidelines are aimed at realizing the UN Sustainable Development Goals (SDGs) and the goals set by the Paris Climate Agreement.

> *"Scientific targets for a healthy reference diet are based on extensive literature on foods, dietary patterns, and health outcomes. This healthy reference diet largely consists of vegetables, fruits, whole grains, legumes, nuts, and unsaturated oils, includes a low to moderate amount of seafood and poultry, and includes no or a low quantity of red meat, processed meat, added sugar, refined grains, and starchy vegetables."—The Lancet Commission*

The American Medical Association (AMA) has raised similar concerns (James L Madara, 2020) on the dietary guidelines for Americans. In August 2020, they suggested:

> *"The AMA supports culturally responsive dietary and nutritional guidelines and recognizes that racial and ethnic disparities exist in the prevalence of*

obesity and diet-related diseases such as coronary heart disease, cancer, stroke, and diabetes. Dairy and meat products are promoted in federal nutrition policies even though they are not nutritionally required. The AMA notes that Black Americans are at particularly high risk for prostate cancer, colorectal cancer, and cardiovascular mortality, and prostate and colorectal cancers are strongly linked to dairy, processed meat, and red meat consumption. Such products also contribute to cardiovascular risk and are not nutritionally indicated for all diets. Accordingly, the AMA recommends that the DGAC clearly indicate in the Dietary Guidelines for Americans (DGA) that meat and dairy products are optional, based on an individual's dietary needs."—AMA

The Physicians Committee (*American Medical Association Calls for Dietary Guidelines To Indicate 'Meat and Dairy Products Are Optional' To Fight Health Disparities*, 2020) also submitted a letter signed by nearly 500 health care professionals, including 300 physicians. The letter says that the DGAC's scientific report:

"preserves antiquated, racially biased dairy-promoting guidelines, despite clear contributions to health problems that take a disproportionate toll in Black Americans and other demographic groups."

Such an overwhelming consensus on some aspect of nutrition among not just the medical and healthcare community, but professionals from across disciplines, is truly a rarity, but not a black swan event. If so many scientists categorically state that red meats, dairy and meats are bad for health, based on research and evidence, there is every reason to believe that there is some truth in what they are saying. At any rate, these foods should be considered *optional,* is what everyone seems to be emphasizing, as opposed to *recommended,* in the guidelines.

The International Agency for Research on Cancer (WHO-IARC) (WHO, 2015) has classified red meat and processed meat as *"probably carcinogenic"* and *"carcinogenic"* for humans, respectively.

As per a study (Diallo et al., 2018) involving a randomized controlled trial of 61,476 men and women, red meat was found to be responsible for carcinogenesis at several cancer locations. In another study (Cross et al., 2007) of 500,000 people in the 50-71 years age group, statistically significant elevated risks were seen for esophageal, colorectal, liver, and lung cancer, on comparing individuals with the highest quintile to the lowest quintile of red meat intake. Moreover, individuals in the highest quintile of processed meat intake had a 20% higher risk of colorectal cancer and 16% higher risk of lung cancer.

A study on the impact of change of diets (Farchi et al., 2017) from red meats to a Mediterranean diet in Italy estimated that if people switched from beef to the Mediterranean diet, a cumulative 5 million years of life lost over the next 18 years could be saved and that life expectancy could be increased by over 7 months for future generations on average.

In some recent research (Osman et al., 2018) another threat has been identified from imported meats, as carriers of pathogens. Certain genuses of *Bacillus* are considered as pathogens for humans, and pose a great health risk. Samples of raw chicken meat and beef meat were found to be carrying enterotoxigenic virulence genes and exhibiting phenotypic virulence characteristics. They pose an epidemiological and health hazard, especially by importing pathogens not found in the country they are being imported into.

In another study (Zhong et al., 2020), it was found that red meats and processed meats are the biggest culprits in other diseases as well. In this cohort study of 29,682 US adults it was observed that intake of processed meat, unprocessed red meat, or poultry was significantly associated with incident cardiovascular disease and that the intake of processed meat or red meat was also associated with all-cause mortality. This has severe health implications for the public. As if this was not convincing enough, in yet another study (Kmietowicz, 2017), of half a million people, red meat was found to be associated with high mortality risks from all causes.

> *"The chances of dying from cancer, heart disease, respiratory disease, stroke, diabetes, infections, kidney disease, or liver disease all increased in line*

There is worse news yet. Another study (Khambadkone et al., 2020) has reported that nitrated meats are shown to be associated with mania in humans and altered behavior and gene expression in rats. Mania is a neuropsychiatric condition associated with morbidity and mortality. It was found that a history of eating nitrated dry cured meat was strongly associated with mania in humans. Feeding the same type of nitrated meat to rats resulted in a human-like bipolar disorder, and changes in intestinal microbiota. These findings have raised alarms on what we are eating, and what it might be doing to our bodies, combined with an urgent need to understand these associations of health diseases with red meats better through more rigorous research.

If you are wondering why you did not already know this (if you didn't), you might want to consider that most of the meat processing companies are giants with huge market control and with significant might to sway public sentiment, opinion and habit-forming decisions. Meats are heavily subsidized and advertised to be enticing to a consumer in the USA. Outside USA is not too different either. The global meat industry is a 1 trillion $ market. The trailblazing book *Meatonomics* (David Robinson Simon, 2013) discusses this at great length. When you can eat cheap meat which your tongue relishes for just a few dollars, why would anyone want to shell out double that amount to buy organic, wholesome vegetables and fruits? Why indeed?

The latter question is the one that is answered in *this* book—*why indeed.*

The cost of meat is paid not just by the environment and animals and birds and bees but directly by your own body. You are paying for meat intake with your own life years.

In a time when plant-based foods, including engineered lab-grown plant-based "meats" are readily available, there is little reason remaining to consume such high levels of meat, especially red meats like beef. Plant-based foods have been recommended in the dietary guidelines of most countries as a healthy choice. There is also some additional good news there...

Anti-aging is all the rage today. Not only are there new technological innovations every few weeks to take strides towards that ambitious goal, but the goals themselves are getting bigger. But there is a very tiny secret to anti-aging which ancient Indians knew, and modern science has begun to discover: ***plant-based foods.***

Telomeres are segments of DNA at the tail end of our chromosomes. As the chromosomes divide when we grow, the telomeres keep getting shorter, normally. They are like the caps on the chromosome ends, which protect the chromosomes from damage, wear and tear. As they get shorter, the chromosomes get more and more open to damage. An enzyme called Telomerase, which is responsible for adding new telomeres at the end of chromosomes upon multiplication, to keep the lengths long. If your body is low on Telomerase, your longevity keeps getting lower and vice versa, if your body has plenty of Telomerase, you will gain longevity and even anti-aging. As such, telomere length is a biomarker for aging.

Oxidative stress can shorten telomeres length, and antioxidants can increase it. In a recent study (Min & Min, 2017) of a representative sample of 3660 US adults, the association between leukocyte telomere length and blood carotenoid levels was studied. It was found that: *"increasing levels of blood carotenoid were significantly associated with longer leukocyte telomeres in US adults. High intake of carotenoid-rich food may play a role in protecting telomeres and regulating telomere length."* Carotenoids are found in plant-based foods like fruits and vegetables, which lend the foods their color. A study in 2008 (Ornish et al., 2008) found that just 3 months of plant-based diet had shown significant change in telomeres activity. A follow up study in 2013 (Ornish et al., 2013) showed a marked increase in the telomere length in the treatment group. Thus, the effects of the change are sustained in the long term upon a switch in the lifestyle change, and is significant.

So there is more than a little reason to switch to plant-based diets, after all. It's where everyone wins.

Bad for the Pests, Worse For You

Pesticides in food are a public health issue that is largely ignored by both, agriculturists and health industry. Either economic viability, crop yields, or other rationale of feasibility are used to justify their use, glossing over the immense damage to the environment and to health of individuals. There is one fundamental question to ask here: when rat poison and other types of poisons that kill animals are poisonous to human beings, why would we allow poisons that kill insects and other creatures near our food supply? Why would someone not perform thorough research on the effects of pesticides on human beings before putting them in our food? Doesn't all commonsense point to a very high probability of these chemicals having an adverse impact on human beings too?

If the argument is to increase yield of crops, we need to extend that argument further. We need to increase yield so we can increase food supply. We need more food supply so that people do not go hungry. We don't want people to die of hunger. But when did it become okay, and acceptable, for people to die of poisons and toxins? If pesticides in food are toxic, but increase yields and food supply, we have a huge supply of toxic food. Have we simply swapped the modes of destroying lives, instead of finding a sustainable solution?

The logic is simple. **Just because we are hungry does not mean we will eat poison.** So, all arguments of crop yields and food supply end right there. It does not matter whether the yield from farming systems that do not use chemicals is 2% lower or 50% lower. It does not matter if the GDP goes down. GDP does not measure many of the costs to the environment. It does not include opportunity costs and externalities. Yields can be improved with time. But once bees become extinct, we cannot bring them back. Once the rain forests dry up, we cannot re-forest them.

The threats to health posed by chemical pesticides are very real and measurable. What is surprising though is that the masses are not aware of it and the mainstream media doesn't want to talk about it. But the facts tell a grim story.

Pesticides gained a huge momentum since 1945, as a by-product of the biowarfare innovations of World War II. In the wake of the war, there was hunger and poverty all over the world and the high demands for immediate supply of food led to the crazed speed of manufacture of pesticides and inorganic fertilizers. Back in the day when DDT was considered a viable option and advertised left, right and center, the seeds of mass poisonings due to pesticides were already sown, and the fruits of that are being reaped to date. This original sin only grew from there.

The worldwide consumption of pesticides is now at 4.12 million tons per year, as of 2018 (FAO 2021). In 1945, this figure was at 50 million kg of pesticides applied worldwide per year (David Pimentel, 2001). This is a 75-fold increase in consumption; that's 7500% increase. In 1973, there were 500,000 cases of pesticide poisoning, with 6000 deaths per year. As per WHO statistics, the numbers stood at 3 million cases of pesticide poisoning worldwide and 220,000 deaths per year, with 735,000 cases of chronic illnesses, as of 2001. Children are the worst affected by pesticide poisoning, since their brain is a much bigger proportion of their body weight compared to adults, and hence, the effect of the pesticide can be that much more pronounced. As of 2001, approximately 40% children working on farms in California showed signs of pesticide poisoning.

It often takes a long time to establish the causality of a disease back to the usage of pesticides, and due to this, worldwide data on pesticide poisoning is patchy and not regularly updated or even available. One example of an alarmingly high percentage of pesticides in drinking water is that of Kerala, India: a woman was found to have levels of Endosulfan in her drinking water that were 900 times of acceptable limits.

Pesticides can cause a big list of diseases, including but not limited to cancer, diabetes *mellitus*, respiratory disorders, neurological disorders, reproductive syndromes and stress. The

'International Agency for Research on Cancer' (IARC) has classified a few pesticides as carcinogens. Several studies (Rani et al., 2021) have shown a heightened risk of bladder cancer and meningioma in men and women who are exposed to pesticides. The levels of organochlorine were shown to be much higher in patients with cancer, as compared with those in a control group in a study performed in Jaipur. While there may not be a huge corpus of research on *every* pesticide in use, the drift is clear: pesticides pose threats to public health, and increased direct exposure to them can be carcinogenic.

Numerous studies confirm a link between pesticides and diabetes (Tyagi et al., 2021), (Park et al., 2019), (Czajka et al., 2019) Farmers who are exposed to pesticides, toxic gases and dust on the farm are also prone to lung diseases, including asthma, bronchitis, organic dust lethal condition, over-sensitivity pneumonitis, silo filler's disorder and neuromuscular respiratory failure. Pesticides can trigger the development of asthma in farmers, with immune disorders, swelling and other complex conditions. Neurological disorders are also a likely side effect of exposure to pesticides, the most common disorders being Alzheimer's and Parkinson's diseases. Scores of studies have established a connection between pesticide exposure and loss of fertility, in both, males and females. Complications with pregnancy have also been reported in women with a prolonged exposure to pesticides.

This is a brief overview of the diseases caused by pesticides. The evidence is pouring in, and more and more research is unraveling this menace, even though common people remain oblivious of the evil since there is not a word on it in mainstream media. Although a high risk for numerous fatal diseases can be seen as an occupational hazard for farmers, there is growing evidence of high levels of pesticide residues in food and water as well, leading to toxicity, poisoning, and possibly slow damage to internal organs on prolonged exposure to even small quantities of toxins due to pesticide usage.

Food alone cannot give us health if we do not see what goes on to our plates, where it comes from, how it was got and what it means for those growing it. How can food which has been farmed at the cost of lives of farmers be good for anyone? We claim to be saving lives by growing more food, but the lives of farmers matter too. This is like adding to one end of the equation and subtracting at the other end. We increased yields but in the process ruined our health, and cost people lives. That food has karmic traces, and cannot give us health, as we can already see from the list of diseases and number of cases of poisoning per year. What we eat matters because it is going to become part of our bodies.

Meat Plants are No Swanky Offices

One of the side effects of the COVID-19 pandemic was that it exposed the ugly, grotesque reality of many aspects of our lives that were getting ignored in the humdrum of business as usual. Sometimes the aftershocks help uncover the seamy side of life, and that part is the silver lining to the otherwise menacing threat of a pandemic.

"We're modern slaves" ran the headline in a story by The Guardian (Oliver Laughland & Amanda Holpuch, 2020) on the fate of the workers at a meat plant. By May 2020, already 20 workers in meatpacking factories had died and another 5000 infected with COVID-19. This was just 3 months into the pandemic. By June 2020, this figure stood at 24,000 infections in meatpacking plants in USA, based on FDA reports. In Europe, this figure was 2670 infections in meatpacking plants. The story ran on to explain how Tyson Foods, a $22 billion giant in the USA, did not care about their employees, did not even acknowledge the death of their employees for weeks. Several meatpacking plants shut down in the USA, during the pandemic months, some temporarily and some permanently. Due to fears of shortage of food supplies, an executive order from the then President, mandated that meatpacking plants be opened, and food supplies kept up.

Now, in this scenario, we must first ask why it is important to eat meat at all in a pandemic. Seeing as how meat makes you prone to a gamut of health conditions, it may not be the wisest decision to consume meat when your body is at a high risk of contracting a severe infection. A plant-based diet is likely to keep you healthier. For a second, is it worthwhile to consume meat when it means putting people's lives at risk? Nobody dies of lack of consumption of meat. Millions of vegetarians and vegans the world over are living, breathing examples of this. But the fact remains that USA considered meat supply to be more important than the lives of the workers.

A big chunk of the workforce in the meatpacking industry are immigrants, who are in need of money for survival—mostly people of color. They had little option but to carry on with their jobs, and just pray they don't catch the virus, which, as was rightly observed by the workers, was "in the air" so there was no real way of controlling it.

Pandemic aside, the meatpacking industry is one of the most hazardous workplaces in the Unites States. As per news reports (Andrew Wasley et al., 2018), second degree burns, amputations, fractured fingers, musculoskeletal disorders, high noise levels, biological hazards of handling live animals and head trauma are just some of the occupational hazards of working at a meatpacking plant (*Meatpacking – Hazards and Solutions | Occupational Safety and Health Administration*, n.d.) in the USA. Compared with the average American worker, the US meat worker is three times more likely to suffer serious injuries. This is worse for beef and pork workers, who are *seven times more likely to suffer repeated injuries.* As per Occupational Safety and Health Administration (OSHA) reports, there are at least 17 "severe" incidents per month at a meatpacking plant. From 2015 to 2017, there were 270 incidents in a 31-month period. These incidents involved amputations, lost limbs and/or damage to fingers. But this is not the end of the tribulations of the meat workers. The meatpacking industry has been shown to cause severe health conditions, which can leave **workers permanently disabled,** and unable to do any work for the rest of their lives. This has economic costs as well. For example, just the Carpal Tunnel syndrome costs 2 billion $ annually (Dale et al., 2013) to the economy (this figure is for all industries).

There is a constant demand to increase line speeds in the pork and beef plants, to escalate the speed of production of meats. These high speeds pose a real threat to the workers, who are at a heightened risk of debilitating injuries from working on the line. It is just the greed for more, more, more meat and money every day that could want to push the limits of speed at the cost of human lives.

Cheap food, high profits, fast.

By virtue of working with live animals, the workers are at a much higher risk (Thin Lei Win, 2020) of other outbreaks like the swine flu, avian flu, and of the zoonotic viruses spilling over to humans after mutation. Workers in meatpacking plants often work elbow to elbow in cold, damp conditions. The plants contain *dead things, along with feces, blood and dirt.* **Who in their right mind would believe that the meat of a dead animal will not be liable to spread infections?**

Working on Blue Floors

Working in a leather tannery is no way better than working in a slaughterhouse; you may not have to slaughter animals (though sometimes tannery workers do boil them and flay them alive), but you do have to deal with a cocktail of chemicals every day, inhale toxic fumes, and work in an extremely unhygienic environment, surrounded by rotting hides and a chemical miasma.

Beyond just the negative sensory overload, there are serious consequences to working in the leather industry. This is no small matter, since this implies a health hazard to a huge number of people. India alone employs about 4 million people in the leather industry, of which approximately 55% are below 35 years of age. Pakistan employs a million people in the leather industry. Bangladesh employs roughly 0.5 million people in the industry, with many of the workers being underage. So, when we say that it is important to take cognizance of the working conditions in the leather industry, it is because it impacts millions of lives directly, and a few more millions indirectly.

Research in the last decade, along with field reports by journalists, have brought the reality of the working conditions industry to light, even though it still remains largely ignored by the masses and policymakers. A few laws were implemented in the last two decades, in different countries, banning a few dyes, and mandating treatment of water that is discharged, but many of these laws are circumvented or only partly followed. The laws address only symptoms of the problems. By no means do the laws solve the germane problems of the cruelty, toxicity, poor working conditions and environmental hazards of leather. To address all of these, only vegan and synthetic leather options remain viable.

In a study conducted in Swedish tanneries between 1958-99 (Mikoczy & Hagmar, 2005), including 2027 workers, a total of 351 cancer cases were observed. An enhanced risk of prostate cancer was observed, attributable to chemicals used in the industry, many of which are carcinogens or suspected carcinogens, like hexavalent chromium salts, tannins, chlorophenols, aniline dyes, formaldehyde, methyl mercury, arsenic, benzene, and chlorinated organic solvents. Leather dust is also considered a threat, and a possible cause for heightened risk of sinonasal cancer. Since the study was mainly observational, the results are only indicative of a trend.

Another study (Decoufle, 1979) conducted in Buffalo, New York, demonstrated high risk of bladder cancer among men and women who have a history of working in leather plants. In men, high risks of cancers of the larynx and pharynx were also observed, which were not explained by smoking habits. Malignant lymphomas were also observed in men and women. A detailed study of the industry led to the conclusion that the workers are exposed to several carcinogens.

In a controlled study of bladder cancer in Massachusetts, the overall risk among male workers in leather plants (adjusted for age and cigarette-smoking habits) was approximately twice that of other occupations.

Leukemia has been observed in leather factory workers in Italy and Turkey. A high risk of bladder cancer has also been observed in studies conducted in Great Britain, USA and Holland.

The damaging effect of the working environment in leather tanneries is not limited to cancers. Another study conducted on rats in India(Kumar et al., 2008) demonstrates that the contaminants from the leather industry can be "Endocrine Disrupting Chemicals" or EDCs. EDCs are environmental contaminants that can alter the normal functioning of the endocrine and reproductive systems, by mimicking or thwarting hormonal actions or altering the way hormones are produced in the body. EDCs can be damaging in low quantities too, if the person is exposed to them for extended periods of time. They can alter the hormonal balance in the body, compromise reproductive fitness, or, worse, can lead to carcinogenesis.

Apart from cancers and exposure to EDCs, there is also the immediate question of inhuman working conditions and threat to life. In many tanneries, workers work without boots and gloves. They climb barefoot into drums with chemical solvents. Child labour is common. Children as young as 10 yrs of age can be seen working with hides and operating heavy machinery, stirring drums with chemicals and one wonders if they have any idea of the dangers to their life. Sulphuric acid can be found in some of the chemicals used in some parts of the tanning process, and workers who are without PPE (personal protective equipment), can get serious skin burns, boils or skin diseases if they are in direct contact with the acids. These slurries also give out toxic fumes. In 2015, three workers in India died after inhaling toxic gases while cleaning one of the drums in a tannery. They were not wearing any PPE. In January 2015, ten workers who were sleeping in a room next to a tank died in an accident where the wall of the room collapsed. They drowned in the effluents of the tanning process.

Sadly, this is not where the health hazards of leather end. There's more.

In Bangladesh, tannery waste is used as a feed on poultry farms (Shams et al., 2009). Scraps of hides that are waste from tanneries are fed to chickens, that are later sold in meat markets. Chromium from tannery wastes thus enters the food chain through poultry meat. Chickens who were fed tannery wastes were found to have deposits of Chromium up to 76 times higher than acceptable range of deposits. Chromium compounds act as carcinogens. These compounds are not destroyed by cooking, boiling or any other way, and hence, humans are exposed to a very high percentage of chromium through their food, thanks to the wastes from tanneries.

Most of the workers affected by the terrible working conditions in leather plants and tanneries belong to the lower stratum of the society, economically speaking. A big percentage are migrant workers, who have moved from villages to cities to find jobs. They are so poor, that if they do get any fatal disease or develop a health condition due to the bad working conditions, they have no means to get medical treatment, healthcare, nor have anyone to look after them. Many of them will lose the main wage earner in the family, should the person be rendered unfit for work due to a health condition. Thus, the leather industry is damaging for both: development as well as environment. The economic growth achieved through the industry is at the cost of the health, wellbeing and living conditions of poor people. It is not only cruel to animals, it is extremely exploitative to those from a financially weak background.

In spite of persistent lobbying for improving work conditions in the industry by international organizations, little has been achieved. Even after enforcing PPE, banning child labour and enforcing water treatment before disposal, the basic working conditions, side effects and aftereffects of the industry do not change. There are certain tasks that are inherently dangerous,

PPE or no PPE. It is the industry which needs to transform fundamentally, and move away from animal-based leather, to plant based or synthetic leathers. At the same time, the international demand for animal leather needs to reduce too. The demand for animal-based leather comes from developed or rich countries. It is fulfilled, in great part, by developing countries. Thus, the cost of the industry to economy, health and environment gets externalized. A person in Italy carrying a fancy handbag made of leather from Kanpur never gets to see or hear about the 12 year old boy who developed skin burns while working at the tannery, nor gets to see or hear the toxic water dumped into Ganga, the most sacred river of India, every day. These externalities cannot be balanced by the money earned by developing countries. It destroys the lives of people and the environment in an irreparable way, and by the time we wake up to the gross injustice of this, it may just be too late to fix it. The time to fix it is now.

Cow, A Pharmacy on Legs

We know that the cow is sacred, but what is it that makes the cow different from other animals? In Hinduism, every animal is sacred in some way or the other, but cow is the most sacred of all animals. Cow is the only animal whose every "produce" is useful to mankind. Every item the cow gives has a practical utility value. This is what made the cow a pivotal part of the agrarian society of India since ancient times. Most of the essential needs of a farmer were taken care of by the produce from the cow, bullocks and calves. In the prospering agrarian society of Vedic times, not only the cow, but the bullocks and calves also had an important place, and were nurtured, rather than seen as a financial burden.

Ayurveda is a holistic science which treats human beings, not the symptoms of the diseases. Ayurvedic medicines are of many types, ranging from ingestible food items to ointments, to poultice, pastes, soups, enemas, incense etc. Till a few decades ago, simple, basic knowledge of Ayurveda was a part of the lifestyle of Hindus. Till a decade ago, kids in Indian households were administered indigenous soups when they were ill, and homemade ointments were applied on wounds, cuts and insect bites. Till one generation ago, the fundamentals of Ayurveda were not something outlandish or "orthodox" or "backward," or "alternative medicine" but rather, the first line of defense against disease. Pills were only when you got really sick and needed immediate treatment.

The *desi* cow, or *Bos indicus*, is the species that is native to India since ancient times. This is the species that is worshiped by Hindus, and whose produce carries innumerable benefits for mankind. Other cow breeds may or may not have the same benefits in their produce and are not considered as sacred. Thus, everything mentioned in this book is applicable only to the indigenous cows of Akhand Bharat.

The cow produces five main items, together called as *panchgavya:* milk, ghee or *goghrita*(clarified butter), *gomaya* or *gobar* (cow dung), *gomutra* or *gojal* (cow urine), and curd. Apart from these, in the modern day, we have also use items like butter, *paneer,* cheese etc. which come from the primary five items.

It is ridiculous to even point out one or two benefits of the produce of the cow as per Ayurveda, because in Ayurvedic texts, every other preparation utilizes something got from the cow! Many ointments have *goghrita* as the base. Many other preparations use *gobar* or *gomutra* or their ash as a part of the preparation process.

As with all things related to the cow, cow milk has been in the midst of several controversies, especially around the benefits of cow milk to human beings. It is important to understand a few things about the two types of milk from two different species of cows: A1 milk and A2 milk. The milk from indigenous cows is termed as A2 milk, whereas that from other cows, for example, Holstein Friesian, is A1 milk. The difference in chemical composition of A1 and A2 milk makes them very different from the standpoint of nutrition. A2 milk, which is obtained from the *desi* cow, is extolled as the most nutritious and life-giving substance in the Vedas.

यद्वर्चो हिरण्यस्य यद्वा वर्चो गवामुत

सत्यस्य ब्रह्मणो वर्चस्तेन मा स सृजामसि |

Sama Veda, Aranyak Parva, Chapter 6, Part 4, Verse 10

"The *tejas* present in gold, cows and the knowledge of truth is what we desire to receive"

"*Tejas*" refers to a certain type of life-giving energy.

In Mahabharat, the merits of the items got from the cow are described in glowing words by Bhagvaan Baldev thus:

कल्य उत्थाय यो मर्त्यः स्पृशेद् गां वै घृतं दधि |

सर्षपं च प्रियङ्गुं च कल्मषात् प्रतिमुच्यते ||

Mahabharat, Daan-Dharma Parva, Chapter 126, Verse 18

"The human being who wakes up in the morning and touches the cow, ghee, curd, big mustard or black mustard seeds, is free of any bad karma."

Modern medicine is yet to catch up with the benefits of the items got from the cow, for the simple reason that insufficient research has been performed on the healing properties of these items. A lot of the available research is on the western breeds of cows, like the Jersey cows, and hence not entirely conclusive when applied to the Vedic society and cownomics. The available research, however, clearly, and unequivocally points to the benign effects of cow milk, cow urine, cow dung, and *panchagavya* on multiple health conditions, including cancer.

Even before treatment is given, the Vaidya (physician), as per Charaka Samhita, is meant to keep the cow as one of the sacred entities on his right, alongside the gods and Brahmins (those dedicated to the knowledge of the *brahman* and sharing that knowledge with the world). This indicates that the presence of the cow was absolutely essential for a Vedic doctor to give any healing services to a patient. It also suggests that the cow was always available at the *vaidyashaala* (hospital-cum-pharmacy).

The Charaka Samhita gives innumerable medicinal benefits of *desi* cow milk, ghee, curd, *gomaya* and *gomutra*. They are used in combinations in all forms of Rasaayana (medicines) – decoctions, poultice, surfactant, fluid for *basti* (enema), soups, snuffs, anointments, fumigants and other edible and non-edible medications. Many herbs and complex preparations are fried or cooked in ghee. Milk is used standalone and as an additive in medications. These are medicines for health conditions like infertility, fevers, infections, disbalance of humours, disorders of the reproductive system, insanity, epilepsy and many more.

Charaka Samhita outlines the process of preparation, benefits of, and application of Rasaayana, which are preparations that not only heal the body from multiple disorders, but prevent many diseases. Most of the Rasaayanas include milk, ghee and curd in the process of preparation. Brahma Rasaayana, Chyavanprasha, and Amalaka Rasaayana are a few examples.

Panchgavya Ghrita, a special formulation described in the Charaka Samhita comprising ghee, cooked with milk, sour curd, *gomutra* and *gobar* juice, is mentioned as an alleviator of jaundice, fever and epilepsy. Panchagavya Ghrita has also been mentioned by Punarvasu as the alleviator of the great disease called attachment to unreality, wherein the person's intellect is masked with *rajas* (the quality leading to restlessness) and *tamas* (the quality leading to depression and lethargy), and who is confused, having little sense, misinterprets eternal and non-eternal and wholesome and unwholesome.

Similar preparations of Mahapanchagavya Ghrita, Mritprasha Ghrita, Amritaprasha Ghrita, Swadamstradi Ghrita, are also described, which are all decoctions in ghee cooked with herbs and fruits of other plants.

Though the amount of research available for these type of treatments is limited, there is plenty of evidence to prove that the treatment of chronic health conditions is possible in Ayurveda, and has been effective.

Gomutra or Cow Urine as a Therapeutic Agent

Amongst the many substances given by the cow, cow urine or *gomutra* is the most effective, and most commonly used in curing chronic diseases and health conditions. *Gomutra* doesn't just help in managing health conditions, but rather curing them from the root, unlike allopathy and modern medicine.

One of the most trailblazing inventions of the last few decades is the effective usage of *gomutra* in the treatment of chronic health conditions like cancer.

Gomutra is also a bioenhancer in the treatment against bacteria and other infections. As per statistics of 2015 (Randhawa & Sharma, 2015), in the USA alone, approximately 2 million people suffer from infections by antibiotic resistant bacteria, of which approximately 23,000 die per year. Many times, the drugs administered for fighting infections prove ineffective, and unnecessarily load the system with chemicals which are not required. This is where cow urine is different. Cow urine comprises (US 6410059 B1) 95% water, 2.5% urea, minerals, 24 types of salts, hormones, and 2.5% enzymes. It also contains iron, calcium, phosphorus, carbonic acid, potash, nitrogen, ammonia, manganese, iron, sulphur, phosphates, potassium, urea, uric acid, amino acids, enzymes, cytokine and lactose. It also contains traces of silver and gold ash. Its chemical composition is very close to the chemicals found in the human body, and hence, consuming cow urine does no damage to the body. Au contraire, it helps restore balance to the body.

Cow urine finds use in therapy for a wide variety of health conditions, and is truly, a "wonder drug." Since much of this treatment happens through Ayurvedic centers, who do not have access to good infrastructure for scientific research, much of this therapy has remained hidden from the rest of the world, and been mocked, ridiculed and derided at will. Yet, the possibilities of treatment with cow urine are endless. Although a few of its uses are discussed here, this is by no means comprehensive or complete.

A research paper by the *Journal of Pharmacy Research* (R et al., 2010) establishes cow urine concentrate as a potent agent with antimicrobial and anthelmintic activity. The research was performed on an indigenous cow breed (Amrit Mahal), using CUC (cow urine concentrate), obtained after distillation of cow urine. The research pointed to clear inhibition of fungal, microbial and worm activity, when subjected to contact with CUC.

Another research (Hoh & Dhanashree, 2017) paper points to considerable effect of cow urine on the Candida species of fungi, inhibiting their growth. Candida is responsible for many common diseases and health conditions. Newly emerged research (Dhama et al., 2005) now also proves the efficacy of cow urine in treating cancer.

A traditional preparation of cow urine (Jarald et al., 2008) with certain herbs was used to treat diabetes in a sample of rats. To study the effect of cow urine, the results of the cow urine preparation were compared with the results of a water-based preparation with the same herbs. The cow urine formulation showed better results than the water-based preparation. Fresh cow urine, without herbs, was also found to have an anti-diabetic effect.

In a study in Europe (Dutta et al., 2006)the anticlastogenic (inhibiting the damage to chromosomes, reducing tumors) effect of cow urine was studied in human peripheral lymphocytes (HPNL) challenged with manganese dioxide and hexavalent chromium. It was found that redistilled cow urine distillate (RCUD) possesses strong antigenotoxic and anticlastogenic properties against HPNLs and HLC treated with Cr+6 and MnO2. This property is mainly due to the antioxidants present in RCUD.

In a study in India (Sathasivam et al., 2010),antimicrobial properties of cow urine were analyzed against Bacillus subtilis, Pseudomonas aeruginosa, Klebsiella pneumoniae and Salmonella typhi. Cow urine was found to be an effective anti-fungal and antibacterial agent. Another studyfound cow urine to be an effective agent to combat multi-drug resistant pathogens.

There are patents (US6410059B1, US6896907B2) on cow urine formulations as well.

Cow urine has diverse uses, beyond just the known sphere of medical treatments. A lot more research is needed to fully evaluate its properties.

Milk as a Therapeutic Agent

Cow milk is extolled in the Vedas as an elixir of life. Ayurveda uses cow milk as a base for numerous formulations. Apart from its nutritious attributes, cow milk has distinct properties which give it therapeutic properties as well.

In a study (Pan et al., 2013), the effect of bovine lactoferrin, a glycoprotein present in milk, was analyzed for its efficacy to combat gastric cancer. The researchers prepared a series of peptide fragments derived from bovine lactoferrin and evaluated their anticancer potency toward the gastric cancer cell line. The study found that lactoferrin could be potentially used as an agent to treat gastric cancer.

In another study (W. Bellamy et al., 1992), a range of bacteria were found to be susceptible to inhibition and inactivation by lactoferricin B, a peptide produced by gastric pepsin digestion of bovine lactoferrin, found in milk. Candida albicans, another pathogen, was found to be highly susceptible to inhibition and inactivation by lactoferricin B, a peptide produced by enzymatic cleavage of bovine lactoferrin, in yet another study (Wayne Bellamy et al., 1993).

Although the therapeutic potential of ghee, panchagavya (Raut & Vaidya, 2018) and other items from the cow have not been evaluated much through modern science, there is copious literature in Ayurveda that gives treatments based on cow products, for a gamut of diseases and health conditions, ranging from fever and headache to dementia.

One chapter in this book is in no way sufficient to fully describe or capture the efficacy of the produce of the cow. Sushrut Samhita, Charak Samhita and other ancient treatises on Ayurveda elaborate these. What is needed is a spotlight on these indigenous methods of healing. Unfortunately, Indian scientists blatantly refused to perform such research (Chandrashekhar, 2020), deriding this science. It is difficult to prove anything, when people do not want to evaluate it. The science of Ayurveda does not need reinvention. It does not require validity for those simple people who know it works because they have seen it passed down through generations. But for the rest of the world, for it to be accepted and embraced, and respected, it requires basic scientific research. The methods, philosophy and concepts of Ayurveda are different from that of Allopathy, but the results can still be evaluated through randomized controlled trials are other empirical methods which establish the efficacy (or lack thereof) of a treatment.

The cow is, for all intents and purposes, a pharmacy on legs. It is up to us humans to tap into this limitless potential of health and healing.

A (Very) Short History of Slaughterhouses in India

At this point, you may be wondering: *how did it come to this?* Where did all these slaughterhouses come from? Was India always this way?

We know enough about European and American history to understand that in the western culture, meat eating and slaughter of cattle were a part of their diet and lifestyle for atleast two centuries. So, the exponential growth in meat consumption visible today is merely a growth in numbers and demand, not a change in the intrinsic character of the countries for the last two centuries. It is a quantitative change, not a remarkable qualitative change.

But this is not the case for India. Ancient Indians ardently worshiped the cow and the Hindu law prohibited cattle slaughter. The karma of cattle slaughter as per Hindu texts was immense, and as such, this crime was prohibited by law in Hindu kingdoms.

This is described in the Mahabharat as the fate that befalls a person who abuses the cow:

पादमुद्यम्य यो मर्त्यः स्पृशेद् गाश्च सुदुर्मतिः ।

ब्राह्मणं वा महाभागं दीप्यमानं तथानलम् ।। २९ ।।

तस्य दोषान् प्रवक्ष्यामि तच्छृणुध्वं समाहिताः ।

आजन्मनां शतं चैव नरके पच्यते तु सः ।

निष्कृतिं च न तस्यापि अनुमन्यन्ति कर्हिचित् ।। ३२ ।।

Mahabharat, Daan-Dharma-Parva, Chapter 126, Verse 29, 32

"The foolish person who kicks a cow, a holy Brahmin, or a flame of fire—I am telling you the fault of such a person, listen carefully...Such a person is cursed to live in Naraka Loka for a hundred janmas. Rishis never accept any gifts from such a person."

So then, how did India become a top exporter of beef, and why is cattle slaughter not already banned all over India?

To answer that question in a fair way, we need to rewind the clock by at least 150 years.

In the 18th century, the "Mohammedans," or the descendants of the Islamic invaders, had brought with them a culture of barbarity to India, one of the aspects of which was widespread meat eating. Combined with severe shortages of food and frequent famines and droughts, the consumption of meat started to become visible in India. At what point Hindus switched to this dietary pattern is unclear. There is no clear documentation or evidence of the dietary patterns of Hindus of this era. But it is well-known that at the time when the British colonialists were spreading through India, a big percentage of Hindus of India were still vegetarian, and it was considered offensive to ask a Hindu to eat meat. The British soldiers often found it difficult to obtain meats for their daily consumption. Cow slaughter was considered equivalent to a slur or curse. There was frequent animosity between the Mohammedans and Hindus on the issue of cow slaughter.

Throughout the course of the 19th century, the Hindus agitated all over India, demanding the ban of cow slaughter in India. In 1800, the number of British soldiers in India was 20,000. By 1856, this number had grown to 45,000 and by 1858, there were 100,000 British soldiers in India. It is well known that the British were habituated to their lifestyle of consuming beef. With troops of British soldiers in India, beef had to be produced from somewhere. It must be noted, that India is a hot country, with a climate which the British did not find easy to adjust to. So, the soldiers in India were already living in a state of "hardship" and as such, the British wanted to find means to keep the spirits of their soldiers high as well. As per the rough estimates of Sri Dharampal, the number of such cattle slaughters would have increased by atleast five to ten-fold from 1800 to 1900. As per reports of Sri Mohandas Gandhi in 1917, an estimated 30,000 cows were being killed every day by the British, for beef.

The British adopted a policy of listening to the demands of the Hindus in modicums—fulfilling what they wanted in part, so as to pacify them, and finding alternate ways to carry out what the British wanted, namely, establish slaughterhouses in India. They achieved this by *refusing to pass any law against cow slaughter,* and giving verbal assurance to the Rajahs of India that they would avoid cow slaughter "as far as possible."

This is from the letters of Warren Hastings, referring to his correspondence with the Rajah of Jodhpur in 1780:

> *"One of his requests is that no cows may be killed in his country. I am sorry that this delicacy was not observed before it was suggested." (Dharampal & T. M. Mukundan, 2002)*

Hindu kings had been in constant correspondence with British officials to ban cow slaughter in India since the 18th century, when the British were already slaughtering cows, against the Hindu religious sentiments.

This is from the letters of C. T Metcalfe to J Adam, Secretary to Governor General in 1818:

> *"I take the opportunity of mentioning in this place, that in the negotiation which I have yet had with the Rajpoot states, they have all sought to have an agreement included in the treaties against the slaughter of horned cattle in their territories. Though I have uniformly declared it to be impossible to*

admit such a stipulation into a treaty, I have assured them that all possible attention shall be paid to their religious feelings on this point." (Dharampal & T. M. Mukundan, 2002)

This gives a drift of the official British stance to a law banning cow slaughter.

The other extremely important, but oft overlooked fact about cow slaughter in India during the British rule is **the pivotal role it played in India's struggle for freedom.** India's First War of Independence in 1857 was first triggered by usage of cow fat in the cartridges of the guns used by British soldiers. At that period, it must be noted, even Brahmins were a part of the British army, and they took deep offense at this slight to their beliefs. The war of 1857 shook the British empire to its roots, and they understood the might of the people of India, should they choose to resist force and brutality. Since the war of 1857, the British revisited and revised their strategy and policy towards handling resistance in India. Instead of using force, they resorted to diplomacy. But it is imperative to understand that this switch in policies was not incidental, but a planned move, because the British colonialists understood that they can be uprooted by Indians if the Indians get organized across the country. The 1857 war could not succeed because it was sporadic and not well planned.

All throughout the 19th century, Hindus were getting aggravated by the callous attitude of the British towards ow slaughter, and they were getting more and more organized around the *Gau Raksha* movement, spearheaded by Swami Dayanand Saraswati, the founder of Arya Samaj, a sect in Hinduism, and supported by the Maharajah of Benares. Hindu leaders and Gurus printed pamphlets on *Gau Raksha* movement and the memorial against kine-killing, and distributed them across towns and villages, traveling by foot. Hindu Rajahs persistently built pressure on the British officials to bring about a law to ban cow slaughter. There were clashes in localities where Mohammedans lived in big numbers, over cow slaughter, especially in open spaces in full view of the public. In these conflicts, the Englishmen invariably backed the Mohammedans, who they believed were more "loyal" to them.

Hindu leaders organized *Gaurakshini Sabhas* all over India, which demonstrated against the British policy of purchasing and slaughtering cows for their troops. *'In November 1889, the campaign by a Gaurakshini Sabha at the Sonepur Fair made it impossible for the Commissariat at Dinapore to purchase cattle for killing for beef.'*—Sri Dharampal observes in his accounts. Hindu leaders and *gurus* demonstrated at fairs and markets and connected with the public at these places. *Fairs and markets thus became centers for dissemination of information on the Gau Raksha movement* to the masses from all socio-economic backgrounds, and also staged a loud protest to the British.

These agitations and demonstrations, along with unifying of Hindus on the issue of cattle protection, was spread all over India.

The British were not ignorant of the significance of this movement. In the minutes of Viceroy Landsowne in December 1893, he observes thus:

"The case presents a close analogy to that which has arisen in Ireland, Just as the Home Rule movement was comparatively power less while its supporters limited their demands to political and constitutional reforms; so, I believe, would any purely political movement in India be innocuous while it represented nothing more than the vague political aspirations of the hall educated classes, and asked for nothing more embarrassing than such reforms as the reconstitution of the Legislative Councils, or the amendment of the Arms Act, or the separation of the Judicial from the Executive. But, as in Ireland, the Home Rule movement became really formidable from the moment when Mr. Parnell's sagacity connected it with the Agrarian question, and thereby gave a material interest in Home Rule to every Irish peasant, so in India the unrest and discontent which have found expression in the Congress movement and in other political combinations, will, I am afraid, become infinitely more dangerous now that a

common ground [anti-kine movement] has been found upon which the educated Hindus and the ignorant masses can combine their forces." (Dharampal & T. M. Mukundan, 2002)

He also observes the role of the *Sabhas,* the markets, and the Hindu leaders and Gurus who walked across the country to unite Hindus in the *Gau Raksha* movement:

"Another point which should, I think not be lost sight of is that these Anti-cow-killing Associations are by no means the only element of danger with which we have to contend. The itinerant preachers who traverse the country, passing from fair to fair, are probably more dangerous in disseminating the propaganda of the movement than the local societies with their elaborate rules framed upon European lines, while beyond these vagrant apostles lies the whole machinery of a secret local organisation, working by underground methods, about which we probably know very little, and leaving upon the surface no track or trace of its proceedings. Even if we were successful in crushing the Associations out of existence, and in arresting, or expelling, the most conspicuous missionaries of the movement, there is, I am afraid, too much reason to suppose that it would survive in spite of us." (Dharampal & T. M. Mukundan, 2002)

Thus, a big part of the effort towards India's struggle for freedom rested on the *Gau Raksha* movement that began in the 19th century, and continued through the 20th century. These linkages all over the country gave the most basic foundation to Hindus to demand freedom from an oppressive British empire.

The British, all through the demonstrations played good-cop, bad-cop, hoping to not make any policy which would be considered flagrant. They laid the blame mostly on the Mohammedans, on cow slaughter, who they hired to carry out the job of slaughtering cattle, all the while pretending to pacify Hindus as well. In the words of **Queen Victoria in 1893:**

"The Queen greatly admired the Viceroy's Speech on the cow-killing agitation. While she quite agrees in the necessity of perfect fairness, she thinks the Muhammadans do require more protection than Hindus, and they are decidedly by far the more loyal. Though the Muhammadan's cow-killing is made the pretext for the agitation, it is, in fact, directed against us, who kill far more cows for our army, than the Muhammadans." (Dharampal & T. M. Mukundan, 2002)

So, it is incontrovertible that the British established slaughterhouses all across the country, especially in locations away from the main city, so that it is not immediately visible to the public.

The British left their legacy of cow slaughter in India when they left, and to date, the *Gau Raksha* movement, which is more than a century old, is only maligned and hated all over the world, true to the British colonial narrative, even though *that narrative is more than a century old*, and grew from a racial bias against Indians and political agendas to lay roots in the Indian subcontinent. Notwithstanding, Indians continue to carry out the practice of cow slaughter, not knowing that their own ancestors gave a mighty resistance to the British just to ban that one practice. I'm not sure who had the last laugh, but I suspect, on this matter, the British have left their mark on India in indelible ink, unless the Indian government decides to right this historic wrong, and fulfill the wishes of our ancestors.

India's Stray Cow Problem

The world over people know that India is home to the biggest livestock population in the world. But did you know that *India is home to almost 5 million stray cows?* These are not cows who have escaped. These are cows who have been set free on the roads by their owners because they can no longer give milk. Cow slaughter is banned in many states of India. So the owners of cows found a simple way to pass on their problem to everyone else: letting the cow loose on the roads. It is akin to abandoning a pet dog or cat who has grown up with you, come to think of you as their parents and family. In India, cows are kept as pets, and that is how they relate with you. But because now dairy farmers have started to see cows as sources of milk, when they can't afford to feed the cow and take care of its medical expenses, they abandon them to die in whichever way life will have them.

India's stray cows are an outcome of insane pace of artificial insemination and forced breeding of cows to increase milk supply. In the race to be the world's biggest milk supplier, India has somewhere lost its religiosity and made the holy cow a machine that gives out milk. The cruelty cows experience in India is different from that in western countries, and there is no direct equivalence between the two. Most of the cow owners are small farmers and dairy farmers in India, with not more than 20 cows each. Many of them give injections to the cows to improve the milk yield all their life. They forcefully impregnate cows to continuously keep them in the lactation cycle, so they can get milk. Though many of them don't deny milk to the calves, nor slaughter the calf, yet, they believe that they do not have the economic means to give food and attention to cows and bulls who cannot give milk. So, when the time comes, they let them loose. This is partly because cow slaughter is banned, so people cannot sell cows for slaughter, and partly because some of the cow owners are Hindu and they do not want to slaughter the cow. Yet, at the same, they are so poor that they cannot feed her either. Many farmers live on less than $1 a day in India, with a family of five. In some states, where cow slaughter is as yet not banned, they are sent for slaughter as well. The religiosity is also missing in many states in which Hindus are a minority, or fast becoming a minority. Most of the states where cow slaughter is not yet banned are also the same states where Hindus already are, or are becoming a minority.

Before going further, I also want to point out, that though this is the sad reality of India, it is also home to numerous *gaushalas*, which are humane cow shelters, run by Hindu organizations and Hindu temples, which take care of cows as pets. India is probably home to the highest number of *gaushalas* in the world. By and large Hindus themselves, and Hindu organizations still strongly feel that the cow must be protected, nurtured and worshiped. But in the last few decades, some of the religiosity has been replaced by apathy in the farmers who are going broke or who have no real knowledge of sustainable lifestyle with the cow. Suicides in farmers have made the headlines many times in the last few decades. There are also many large scale dairy farms which do not treat the cow as sacred, but are very much similar to dairy farms of the west. These dairy farms sell cows for slaughter.

These stray cows have a sad life. They wander the roads, eat trash from the road and trash bins. Every Indian would have seen at least a few cows eating plastic and other trash from the roadside at least once in their lives. This is no rarity. It is very common. Once, a vet retrieved 71 kilograms (156.6 pounds) of plastic from the stomach of a pregnant cow ("Vets Pull out 71 Kg of Waste from Stray Cow's Stomach," 2021). The calf could not survive because there was no space for the calf to grow in the cow's womb, so much space was taken up by plastic and other toxic wastes. Both, the cow and calf, died during the surgery and could not be saved. The toxic wastes had to be removed by hand from the cow's body. Cows who roam the roads live in a pitiable state. I wouldn't wish what they go through on my enemies, if I had any.

Many cows walk on the roads and meet with accidents, with no medical attention available to them. Commuters complain, of course, of cows on the road as a "nuisance", but they ignore the fact that it is really not the fault of the cows. They did not ask to be born. They only gave milk to humans their whole life, after which they are abandoned, to fend for themselves. Where are we humans expecting them to go and what are we expecting them to do and eat? It is only normal for a starved animal to want to eat. These cows, in villages, often try to eat the crop of farmers, which aggravates the farmers. But let us remember that the problem is created mainly because we stopped treating cows as the holy cow and mother and started treating her as a milk giving machine. Did we expect that it can somehow lead to a good outcome? It is a karmic cycle. Humans cannot escape the fruits of their cruel actions to other beings. It always boomerangs.

It is appalling that most of mainstream media highlights this as a problem because of ban on cow slaughter. It shows that we are still not looking at the right problem, leave alone finding a solution. In the local language, animal rights' activists are called *"gau rakshaks"* in India—those who have taken the responsibility to protect the cow. They go around giving medical treatment to injured cows and rescuing them to take them to humane cow shelters where they can be fed and nursed back to health. Numerous such small organizations exist all across India, and even by NRIs in the USA, who wear the religion on their sleeve and are willing to take any risks on their own lives to rescue cows.

Saving cows in India is not an easy job, because there are many who have vested interests to capture these cows and sell them for slaughter. There is a huge black market for illegal trade of cows for slaughter. These butchers are always at odds with *gau rakshaks*, and are, for obvious reasons, riled by the presence of *gau rakshaks* who are out to rescue cows. Scuffles sometimes break out, and police is required to intervene. But the mainstream media, which has mis-identified the problem in the first place, demonizes the animal rights' activists who are trying to save injured and tortured animals, instead of the butchers. This is why the world scorns India's cow protection while at the same time ridiculing India for exporting beef. How can you have it both ways? Either respect cow protection and scorn beef exports or scorn cow protection and praise beef exports. But how can such blatant hypocrisy be peddled for decades? Readers do not see through the propaganda; it is so successfully run.

India's stray cattle problem has a direct solution if farmers are taught sustainable living with the cow, for which milk is not even needed from the cow. The separation of farming from the cow is the grassroot problem. When the two became disconnected, over a few decades, knowledge transfer of living sustainably with the cow was not passed on to the next generations, and many farmers of today are living a hand to mouth existence because they are 100% dependent on their crop and are in heavy debts. They do not know organic farming, Ayurvedic health solutions or other numerous ways in which owning a cow can help live respectably, even if she doesn't give milk. Even oxen, who were originally the farmers' best friends, because they helped till the land, are now being sold off to the butchers! Oxen have enough power to run a powerhouse. The manual labour easily possible for them can help people generate power in their own small establishments. India has numerous clean energy solutions in the form of the *gauvansh* (cow, bull or calf), but these solutions are not being implemented on a scale needed to solve the looming problems of stray cattle and cow slaughter.

Some states, like Uttar Pradesh, have ordered a cow protection cess on public companies to raise funds to house rescued cows. UP has also created cow shelters all over the state in buildings that are no longer in use. These are all noble efforts, but they are not run in a sustainable way so as to give a respectable life to the cows and the ones caring for the cows. This book has outlined a plethora of ways how humans can live symbiotically with the cow. Those methodologies need to be implemented. Many cows die of hunger and thirst in state cow shelters or while being transported to cow shelters. Why should it come to this?

India, as the land of sages and the holy Himalayas and the sacred Ganga, should know that its economic prosperity can be revived and restored only when it nurtures cows, not otherwise. The karma of cow slaughter is too huge. As illustrated all throughout the book, karma is not some elusive concept to scare people into good behaviour. It is our own cruelty boomeranging back to us. There is still time. If we want to be saved, we must save the holy cow.

The Holy Cow

Hindus have been labelled and bracketed as "regressive", "orthodox," "blind believers" "cow piss drinkers" and been given many other such pejorative appellations, primarily because we are a civilization who, since the beginning, believe in nurturing, loving and worshipping the cow, and we stuck to this tradition when the "white man" thought it better to slaughter cows and consume their meats and veal as "delicacy." Many across the world today have thankfully woken up to the barbaric cruelty cows receive from humans, and have become vegans, vegetarians or animal rights' activists; yet, **as a people who *worship* the cow, Hindus stand on their own.** We stand apart due to the depth of the emotions we associate with the cow, a "mere animal" as per the rest of the world. Here, I would like to point out, that there is a growing number of "Hindus" who have bought into western ideologies and principles of consumerism and no longer consider the cow as sacred, or are so consumed by their own hedonistic desires and the wish to tantalize their tongues that sacredness goes out of the window when a beef curry is in front of them, but these are not the people I am referring to when I talk of Hindus. Many Hindus today are woefully ignorant about their own culture, scriptures, traditions and heritage, and are Hindus in name only. Worship of the cow is as central to Hinduism as any other tenet like karma, reincarnation, deity worship, Om or our millions of traditions. In short, ***cow worship is inseparable from Hindu Dharma.***

To understand this, we must again go back to the source books, the scriptural texts of Hindu Dharma—it is verily important to understand why Hindu Dharma worships cow, nature, and sees all beings as Divine.

These verses are from the Chandogya Upanishad, Chapter 6, Part 10, Verse 1 and 2. The Chandoya Upanishad reiterates the tenet that in the beginning there was only Consciousness, from which all of life forms manifested. So, all beings are different manifestations of the Cosmic Consciousness. In these verses, the Upanishad specifically explains how all creatures are all manifestations of Consciousness or Divinity:

इमाः सोम्य नद्यः पुरस्तात्प्राच्यः स्यन्दन्ते

पश्चात्प्रतीच्यस्ताः समुद्रात्समुद्रमेवापियन्ति स समुद्र

एब भवति ता यथा तत्र न

विदुरियमहमस्मीयमहमस्मीति

एवमेव खलु सोम्येमाः सर्वाः प्रजाः सत आगम्य न विदुः

सत आगच्छामह इति त इह व्याघ्रो वा सिꣳहो वा

वृको वा वराहो वा कीटो वा पतङ्गो वा दंशो वा मशको वा

यद्यद्भवन्ति तदाभवन्ति ॥

Chandogya Upanishad, Chapter 6, Part 10, Verse 1 and 2

"These rivers run from eastern towards the east and from western towards the west, to the sea. They go from sea to sea, and merging, they become the sea. As those rivers, they do not know, upon merging with the sea, whether they are this or that river. (1)

So also all the creatures, when they come back from the Source, they do not know that they are emerged from the Source. All the creatures here, be it a tiger, lion, boar, wolf, insects, gnat or mosquito, they manifest again and again from That. (2).

This is why *Ahimsa* is a core tenet of Hinduism—because any harm, hurt caused to other creatures is harming your own self, because everything is a manifestation from the same Source. The cow, as mentioned earlier, is the most evolved animal, and as such, bestowed with Divine powers to raise the consciousness of everyone around her. Just keeping company of the cow is enough to help you lose your sense of attachment to your "identity" and blissfully merge with the Divine and realize enlightenment. The Upanishads describe this initiation from the Guru to the seeker as *"Tattvam Asi"—"You are That."*

A remarkable story from the Chandogya Upanishad (Chapter 4; Part 4, Verse 1 to Part 9, Verse 3) illustrates this principle well. The story is of a child, Satyakama. The Sanskrit word *"satyakama"* means "the seeker of Truth." Satyakama did not know who his father was; his mother was named Jabala. He went in search of Guru, to seek the knowledge of the Self or *Brahman—Brahma Vidya—*and approached the great Rishi (sage) Haridrumata Gautam and asked him to give him the knowledge of *Brahma Vidya.* The sage asked him about his *gotra* (lineage). The child honestly answered the sage, that he did not know his *gotra.* But as his mother was called Jabala, he was to be called as Satyakama Jabala. The sage Gautam, on hearing this answer, says that he is truly a Brahmin, for only a Brahmin could give such a truthful answer. He accepted him as his disciple and agreed to teach him. He initiated him to silence of the mind as a meditation. He then entrusted the task of caring for his cows to Satyakama, in answer to his quest. He gave Satyakama 400 lean and thin cows, and asked him to live with the cows in the forest, and return only when the 400 had multiplied into 1000 cows. This is implied to suggest that the sage intended the child to spend a long time with the cows, away from human settlement, immersed in nature. Satyakama accepted this *Guru Vaak* (instruction of the Guru) and set upon his journey with the blessings of his Guru.

In the forest, Satyakama spent all his time with the cows and the animals in the forest. He nurtured the cows and looked after them well. Over a period of time, he developed such a deep, intimate bond with the cows, that all his societal ideas began to melt away, and he became acutely sensitive to other creatures and living beings, being in sync with them, able to understand them and their language. He reached a space of Oneness, from where he could connect with any creature or part of nature, and imbibe the knowledge they had to impart. This was an elevated level of consciousness, which was not otherwise possible in the human society. It was possible because of a deep sense of empathy and connected-ness with all creatures and the Whole. He received knowledge of the Brahman from a bull, a fire, a swan, and a diver bird. Receiving this knowledge, he is reminded by the bull that he now has 1000 cows in his herd and he must go back to his Guru as instructed. By this time, Satyakama had forgotten all about his life before going to the forest and his Guru! When Satyakama goes back to the Guru, Rishi Gautam sees a glowing effulgence in him, and the cows look happy and healthy. The sage knows that Satyakama has already received the knowledge the Guru intended him to receive. He was now ready for receiving the ultimate knowledge, for which he was prepared through his journey. He then instructs him in the remaining knowledge, and completes his initiation with which he realizes the Ultimate as manifest in him, which is the *Brahma Vidya*.

This short story gives insight into what the company of cows and being in tune with nature can do for us, and why it is emphasized in Hindu culture, why we worship the cow. Spending time with cows peels off layers of pain and suffering, societal ideas, which stop us from experiencing the true nature of existence. As such, worship of the cow as an everyday practice was meant to lead people to the Ultimate, enlightenment or Moksha. This is why the cow is holy to Hindus, and is worshipped.

"The future is already here, it's just not evenly distributed"

It would have been impossible for me to explain what the Cownomics model would look like, or how it would function, without first describing every aspect of the meat-dairy-leather industries and the historical and cultural context of the cow. Without that, the Cownomics model, as I am about to propose, would not sound "feasible."

So what does the Cownomics model look like?

"The future is already here—it's just not evenly distributed."—William Gibson, The Economist, December 4, 2003"

In the last decade, there has been a growing movement away from meat and dairy, while veganism has become recognized as a mainstream food choice, even though it is not yet recognized everywhere as a mainstream food choice. Though vegetarians have existed for centuries in India, which is home to more than 400 million vegetarians, until a decade ago, it was mocked and ridiculed as a food choice in countries outside India. In the last 20 years alone, copious scientific literature and research has been produced to highlight all the aspects of the meat-dairy-leather industries, which was neither known, nor on anyone's radar earlier.

Summary: we are getting there, but slowly. We need to pick up the pace, and connect the dots.

The Cownomics Model

I have used the word "model" to signify a prototype and the fundamental unit of our society, which could be of varying scales, from a cluster of 15-20 households to one entire city or one state (like Sikkim) or one whole country (like Bhutan) (Clarissa Wei, 2016). Although even these places are not exactly as per the "model" I will detail, because they lack many of its components, they are the best available laboratories to study how one can begin to implement a Cownomics model, in terms of policy and change of practices.

A Cownomics unit is a self-sustaining unit, which is economically viable and runs based on a symbiotic relationship between its different components. It typically has the following components:

Vaidyashala (Ayurvedic nursing home and pharmacy) with a herb garden—takes *gomutra*, *gobar*, curd, *ghee*, milk from

Gaushala and gives "Cowpathy" treatment for varying health conditions, for both, humans and animals.

Gaushala (Humane cow shelter)—gives milk, *gomutra*, *gobar*, takes in cow feed, water, grazes on the pastures.

Agricultural land with organic farming—takes in organic biofertilizer, *gomutra* as pesticide, seeds, water, energy/electricity; gives organic food, cow feed and other produce.

Grazing pasture—planted with grass and surrounded by trees. Cows graze here.

Rain water harvesting systems and water tank—systems installed in all building structures, walkways, drains, roofs to capture rain water and feed it to one central water tank where it can be filtered and used for domestic or irrigation purposes.

Solar Panels with battery storage—typically installed on roofs, but can also be installed on independent, tree-like vertical posts; gives electricity.

Biogas Digester(s) with plumbing for cooking gas—takes in water, *gobar*, agricultural wastes, night soil, food waste, leaves of trees and other plant wastes and stubble; gives organic biofertilizer and cooking gas.

Power plant—takes in cooking gas produced from biogas digester; produces electricity.

Home crafts Center—take in *gobar*, *ghee*, herbs, curd, milk, nuts, fruits, other produce; produce items of everyday consumption and usage like incense, dried *gobar* cakes, *diyas* (lamps) etc.

Market space—for selling all items produced in every component.

Learning Center—for learning the science, art, craft and plumbing for every component.

All these components function in sync with each other, support each other and are complementary to each other. They form an ecosystem which is sustainable, low cost, can be designed to be economically viable, healthy, and environment-friendly. Modifications, additions and adaptations can be made to the components based on the culture, geography, climate and demography. This is a sketchy outline of the core concept of what is the Cownomics model, and how it would function. It is designed based on the ancient Vedic agrarian, cow-based society, modified for modern technology and upgrades, and current requirements.

In reality, for successful implementation, this will require rigorous research, randomized control trials, and a few prototype models to arrive at the right proportions, sizes and relationship ratios to ensure that the system is 100% sustainable, carbon negative, environmentally nourishing and, ofcourse, humane. This is a draft and an outline, from which at least fifty research studies can be carried out, and will require inputs and contributions of experts across disciplines.

Any city, state, country or locality can build this if they wish to.

Many Gaushalas, cities, farms, independent enterprises, cow shelters etc have implemented parts of this model, in their own way, but because they have not included all the core components, they still have ongoing problems of one sort or another. They have taken the first giant step, but it is possible to make that step into a journey towards a better society. I have attempted to give solutions to the problems I have seen in many existing establishments through this framework.

As of today, a lot of research exists, but for isolated issues and scenarios. There is very sparse economics research on a similar system. Research which empirically evaluates the pluses and minuses of different methods of implementation, of the net carbon emissions, waste management, land productivity, and all other related aspects discussed throughout the length of this book, but in this framework, will be immensely helpful.

I am not suggesting that this is a perfect model. But rather, a skeletal framework, a starting point with brings together all the pluses of a cow-based society and attempts to eliminate all the negatives of the modern day meat-dairy-leather industry, in a modern setting. If this model can be perfected and implemented, there is no reason why the villages of India should remain backwards and under-developed. Over a period of time, the economic gains from nurturing the earth will start to show in balance sheets, and the cycle of growth will be a virtuous one, rather than a vicious one.

After all, this book is meant to be an investigation and inquiry into what a humane society looks like, and how it can be realized without burning every last dollar. The biggest arguments against most plans to check environmental disasters are those of money—"it is too expensive." But if we can arrive at a solution which can be made economically viable, and also achieve all other goals as outlined, then we can say we have a holistic solution which can work in the long term. Otherwise, we are only treating parts of the problem, without ever understanding the whole. If we keep treating the symptoms of the problem, we can never arrive at permanent solutions. Only when we stitch all the bits and pieces together, and see it in one frame, does it all make sense. I have attempted to give that frame.

The cownomics model is a framework of existing, wherein we see experientially that changing the place of the cow in the society can change the society.

A Note of Thanks

I don't know the exact date when I started working on this book, but my records show that I have been working on it since Q3-2018. It's safe to say that I have toiled over this book for 2.5 years, though looking back I wonder where all that time went and wish I had more time so I could add more to this book. But the pen, or keyboard, must stop at some point.*

I have faced troubles of every kind in this period. There are a few people who stood by me like a rock all throughout this period, and believed in me, and the book, much more than I believed in my own self. My family has been a source of constant support to me and without them, I would be nowhere today, literally. Not only did they believe in me, they never let me doubt my own self or let anyone else's antics get to me or deter me from working on this book. There were phases when I was feeling low and when I wondered whether writing this book was worth my while, especially since nobody seemed to care about saving the cow as I did, but the few people around me who did care, made sure I always knew that it is worth it, every bit. Anyone who knows me, will know that I am more or less of an introvert. So, though I do not have an army of friends, the few around me make up in quality what lacks in numbers. I am immensely grateful to all of those friends...you know who you are.

My mother has always been my biggest supporter, no matter what decision I take in life, and I don't know what I would do without her.

My sister is the life support system who has helped me through every trough in the sine wave of life, and this book is no exception. She also helped me with proofreading the book, and I don't know a more articulate person to do that job so sincerely and promptly.

I also want to thank my friend, code name SRS, who with his stories of his childhood spent around cows, and his unwavering compassion for animals, made a lasting impact on me and moved me to not give up when I was feeling dull or exhausted. @SRS, you believed in me, I know. I may not have said it, but it mattered a lot to me, and always will. I hope and pray that you are always happy in life.

I would also like to thank Sri Sanjeev Newar and Sri Vashi Sharma who helped me at every turn with all the resources they had.

I also want to thank all the people who contributed to my fundraiser for the book in 2019. It helped me get through a difficult phase, where I had to procure a lot of books and research papers to work on this project. It's not just the monetary contribution, but the fact that so many people, mostly unknown to me, came forward to support me and believed in me, told me more about the need for the book and the trust people had on me, than any other single event in the last 2 years. Their trust gave me the strength to wake up long nights, to endure the pain, to get back up after facing intermittent failures.

Most of all, I would like to thank YOU, the reader, for deciding to be a part of this story of Cownomics, deciding to be one spark in the fire of architecting a better world, not just for us, but for all creatures.

Last, but definitely not the least, I want to thank Mahadeva and my Guru who sowed the seed of this book in me, then gently led me to all the resources I needed to put it together, and wired my brain to do what is needed in the end. I don't know (and don't really care) how anyone else sees this book, but I know that Mahadeva has manifested something through me which I did not imagine back in 2018 when I took this on. Mahadeva, this book is Your *prasada,* to me, to the world. Let this book become a movement, a sentiment, a lifestyle, with your blessings. ***Shivaya Namah.***

*Or not. Refer to cownomics.com for a continuation of this book, in the form of updates, new articles, research and a lot more.

Cownomics

Bibliography

Abha Chhabra, K. R. Manjunath, Sushma Panigrahy, & J. S. Parihar. (2009). Spatial pattern of methane emissions from Indian livestock on JSTOR. *Current Science*, *96*(5), 683–689. www.jstor.org/stable/24104562

American Medical Association Calls for Dietary Guidelines To Indicate 'Meat and Dairy Products Are Optional' To Fight Health Disparities. (2020, August 14). Physicians Committee for Responsible Medicine. https://www.pcrm.org/news/blog/american-medical-association-calls-dietary-guidelines-indicate-meat-and-dairy-products

Andreas Gattinger, Adrian Muller, Matthias Haeni, Matthias Haeni, Andreas Fliessbach, Nina Buchmann, Paul Mäder, Matthias Stolze, Pete Smith, Nadia El-Hage Scialabba, & Urs Niggli. (2012). Enhanced top soil carbon stocks under organic farming on JSTOR. *Proceedings of the National Academy of Sciences of the United States of America*, *109*(44), 18226–18231. www.jstor.org/stable/41829835

Andrew Wasley, Christopher D Cook, & Natalie Jones. (2018, July 5). Two amputations a week: the cost of working in a US meat plant | Environment | The Guardian. *Guardian.* https://www.theguardian.com/environment/2018/jul/05/amputations-serious-injuries-us-meat-industry-plant

ANNA STAROSTINETSKAYA. (2019, June 6). *Meat Companies Threaten United States with 500 Times More Raw Sewage than New York City Creates | VegNews.* VegNews. https://vegnews.com/2019/6/meat-companies-threaten-united-states-with-500-times-more-pollution-than-new-york-city-creates

Arjen Y. Hoekstra, Ashok K. Chapagain, Maite M. Aldaya, & Mesfin M. Mekonnen. (2011). *The Water Footprint Assessment Manual - Setting the Global Standard.* http://www.fao.org/sustainable-food-value-chains/library/details/en/c/266049/

Bellamy, W., Takase, M., Wakabayashi, H., Kawase, K., & Tomita, M. (1992). Antibacterial spectrum of lactoferricin B, a potent bactericidal peptide derived from the N -terminal region of bovine lactoferrin. *Journal of Applied Bacteriology,* 73(6), 472–479. https://doi.org/10.1111/j.1365-2672.1992.tb05007.x

Bellamy, Wayne, Wakabayashi, H., Takase, M., Kawase, K., Shimamura, S., & Tomita, M. (1993). Killing of Candida albicans by lactoferricin B, a potent antimicrobial peptide derived from the N-terminal region of bovine lactoferrin.

Medical Microbiology and Immunology, *182*(2), 97–105. https://doi.org/10.1007/BF00189377

Bill Winders, & Elizabeth Ransom. (2019). The Global Meat Industry, 1960–2016. In *Global Meat*. The MIT Press. https://doi.org/10.7551/mitpress/11868.003.0004

Borrelli, P., Robinson, D. A., Fleischer, L. R., Lugato, E., Ballabio, C., Alewell, C., Meusburger, K., Modugno, S., Schütt, B., Ferro, V., Bagarello, V., Oost, K. van, Montanarella, L., & Panagos, P. (2017). An assessment of the global impact of 21st century land use change on soil erosion. *Nature Communications*, *8*(1), 1–13. https://doi.org/10.1038/s41467-017-02142-7

Bryngelsson, D., Wirsenius, S., Hedenus, F., & Sonesson, U. (2016). How can the EU climate targets be met? A combined analysis of technological and demand-side changes in food and agriculture. *Food Policy*, *59*, 152–164. https://doi.org/10.1016/j.foodpol.2015.12.012

Budzianowski, W. M. (2011). Can "negative net CO_2 emissions" from decarbonised biogas-to-electricity contribute to solving Poland's carbon capture and sequestration dilemmas? *Energy*, *36*(11), 6318–6325. https://doi.org/10.1016/j.energy.2011.09.047

Chandogya Upanishad (Sanskrit). (n.d.).

Chandrashekhar, V. (2020). Indian scientists decry 'infuriating' scheme to study benefits of cow dung, urine, and milk. *Science*. https://doi.org/10.1126/science.abb4387

Clarissa Wei. (2016, October). *This Man Is Helping the Entire Country of Bhutan Go Organic*. VICE. https://www.vice.com/en/article/wnbxjn/this-man-is-helping-the-entire-country-of-bhutan-go-organic

Cross, A. J., Leitzmann, M. F., Gail, M. H., Hollenbeck, A. R., Schatzkin, A., & Sinha, R. (2007). A prospective study of red and processed meat intake in relation to cancer risk. *PLoS Medicine*, *4*(12), 1973–1984. https://doi.org/10.1371/journal.pmed.0040325

Czajka, M., Matysiak-Kucharek, M., Jodłowska-Jędrych, B., Sawicki, K., Fal, B., Drop, B., Kruszewski, M., & Kapka-Skrzypczak, L. (2019). Organophosphorus pesticides can influence the development of obesity and type 2 diabetes with concomitant metabolic changes. In *Environmental Research* (Vol. 178, p. 108685). Academic Press Inc. https://doi.org/10.1016/j.envres.2019.108685

Dale, A. M., Harris-Adamson, C., Rempel, D., Gerr, F., Hegmann, K., Silverstein, B., Burt, S., Garg, A., Kapellusch, J., Merlino, L., Thiese, M. S., Eisen, E. A., & Evanoff, B. (2013). Prevalence and incidence of carpal tunnel syndrome in US working populations: Pooled analysis of six prospective studies. *Scandinavian Journal of Work, Environment and Health*, *39*(5), 495–505. https://doi.org/10.5271/sjweh.3351

David Pimentel. (2001). Overview of the Use of Genetically Modified Organisms and Pesticides in Agriculture on JSTOR. *Indiana Journal of Global Legal Studies*, 9(1), 51–64. https://www.jstor.org/stable/20643819?seq=1

David Robinson Simon. (2013). *Meatonomics: How the Rigged Economics of Meat and Dairy Make You Consume Too Much.* Conari Press. https://www.amazon.com/Meatonomics-Economics-Consume-Much-Smarter/dp/1573246204/ref=sr_1_1?dchild=1&keywords=meatonomics&qid=1616178527&sr=8-1

Decoufle, P. (1979). Cancer risks associated with employment in the leather and leather products industry. *Archives of Environmental Health*, *34*(1), 33–37. https://doi.org/10.1080/00039896.1979.10667364

Delimaris, I. (2013). Adverse Effects Associated with Protein Intake above the Recommended Dietary Allowance for Adults. *ISRN Nutrition*, *2013*, 1–6. https://doi.org/10.5402/2013/126929

Dhama, K., Chauhan, R. S., & Singhal, L. (2005). Anti-Cancer Activity of Cow Urine: Current Status and Future Directions. *International Journal of Cow Science.*

Dhar, N. R. (1943). Improvement of the nitrogen status of soils and the origin of soil nitrogen. *Nature*, *151*(3838), 590–592. https://doi.org/10.1038/151590a0

DHAR, N. R., & MUKERJI, S. K. (1936). Nitrogen Fixation with Cow-Dung. *Nature*, *138*(3503), 1060. https://doi.org/10.1038/1381060a0

Dharampal, & T. M. Mukundan. (2002). *The British Origin of Cow-Slaughter in India*. Society for Integrated Development of Himalayas. https://www.amazon.in/British-Origin-Cow-Slaughter-India/dp/8187827041/

Diallo, A., Deschasaux, M., Latino-Martel, P., Hercberg, S., Galan, P., Fassier, P., Allès, B., Guéraud, F., Pierre, F. H., & Touvier, M. (2018). Red and processed meat intake and cancer risk: Results from the prospective NutriNet-Santé cohort study. *International Journal of Cancer*, *142*(2), 230–237. https://doi.org/10.1002/ijc.31046

Dixit, S., Yadav, A., Dwivedi, P. D., & Das, M. (2015). Toxic hazards of leather industry and technologies to combat threat: A review. In *Journal of Cleaner Production* (Vol. 87, Issue C, pp. 39–49). Elsevier Ltd. https://doi.org/10.1016/j.jclepro.2014.10.017

Dobson, A. P., Pimm, S. L., Hannah, L., Kaufman, L., Ahumada, J. A., Ando, A. W., Bernstein, A., Busch, J., Daszak, P., Engelmann, J., Kinnaird, M. F., Li, B. v, Loch-Temzelides, T., Lovejoy, T., Nowak, K., Roehrdanz, P. R., & Vale, M. M. (2020). Ecology and economics for pandemic prevention. *Science*, *369*(6502), 379. https://doi.org/10.1126/science.abc3189

Dr Ganga Sahay Sharma. (2017a). *Rigved (Hindi Edition)*. Vishv Books Private Ltd. https://www.amazon.in/Rigved-Hindi-Ganga-Sahay-Sharma-ebook/dp/B075NZ5XKK/

Dr Ganga Sahay Sharma. (2017b). Atharvaved (Hindi Edition). In *Vishv Books Private Ltd.* https://www.amazon.in/Atharvaved-Hindi-Ganga-Sahay-Sharma-ebook/dp/B075MD76FZ/

Dr Rekha Vyas. (2017). Samaveda (Hindi Edition). In *Vishv Books Private Ltd.* https://www.amazon.in/Samaveda-Hindi-Dr-Rekha-Vyas-ebook/dp/B075FDZ9H2/

Dutta, D., Devi, S. S., Krishnamurthi, K., & Chakrabarti, T. (2006). Anticlastogenic effect of redistilled cow's urine distillate in human peripheral lymphocytes challenged with manganese dioxide and hexavalent chromium. *Biomedical and Environmental Sciences*, *19*(6), 487–494. https://europepmc.org/article/med/17319276

Economic Losses, Poverty & Disasters. (2017). https://www.unisdr.org/files/61119_credeconomiclosses.pdf

Farchi, S., de Sario, M., Lapucci, E., Davoli, M., & Michelozzi, P. (2017). Meat consumption reduction in Italian regions: Health co-benefits and decreases in GHG emissions. *PLOS ONE*, *12*(8), e0182960. https://doi.org/10.1371/journal.pone.0182960

Faust, C. L., McCallum, H. I., Bloomfield, L. S. P., Gottdenker, N. L., Gillespie, T. R., Torney, C. J., Dobson, A.

P., & Plowright, R. K. (2018). Pathogen spillover during land conversion. *Ecology Letters*, *21*(4), 471–483. https://doi.org/10.1111/ele.12904

Flower, F. C., & Weary, D. M. (2003). The effects of early separation on the dairy cow and calf. In *Animal Welfare* (Vol. 12, Issue 3, pp. 339–348). Elsevier. https://doi.org/10.1016/s0168-1591(00)00164-7

Garba, J., Samsuri, W. A., Othman, R., & Hamdani, M. S. A. (2019). Evaluation of Adsorptive Characteristics of Cow Dung and Rice Husk Ash for Removal of Aqueous Glyphosate and Aminomethylphoshonic Acid. *Scientific Reports*, *9*(1), 1–10. https://doi.org/10.1038/s41598-019-54079-0

Gerbens-Leenes, P. W., Mekonnen, M. M., & Hoekstra, A. Y. (2013). The water footprint of poultry, pork and beef: A comparative study in different countries and production systems. *Water Resources and Industry*, *1–2*, 25–36. https://doi.org/10.1016/j.wri.2013.03.001

Green, A., Clark, C., Favaro, L., Lomax, S., & Reby, D. (2019). Vocal individuality of Holstein-Friesian cattle is maintained across putatively positive and negative farming contexts. *Scientific Reports*, *9*(1), 1–9. https://doi.org/10.1038/s41598-019-54968-4

Green, R. F., Joy, E. J. M., Harris, F., Agrawal, S., Aleksandrowicz, L., Hillier, J., Macdiarmid, J. I., Milner, J., Vetter, S. H., Smith, P., Haines, A., & Dangour, A. D. (2018).

Greenhouse gas emissions and water footprints of typical dietary patterns in India. *Science of the Total Environment, 643,* 1411–1418. https://doi.org/10.1016/j.scitotenv.2018.06.258

Hannah Ritchie, & Max Roser. (2017, August). *Meat and Dairy Production.* Published Online at OurWorldInData.Org. https://ourworldindata.org/meat-production#beef-and-buffalo-cattle-meat-production

Harris, F., Green, R. F., Joy, E. J. M., Kayatz, B., Haines, A., & Dangour, A. D. (2017). The water use of Indian diets and socio-demographic factors related to dietary blue water footprint. *Science of the Total Environment, 587–588,* 128–136. https://doi.org/10.1016/j.scitotenv.2017.02.085

Harvard Medical School. (2020, March 30). *When it comes to protein, how much is too much? – Harvard Health.* Harvard Health Publishing. https://www.health.harvard.edu/nutrition/when-it-comes-to-protein-how-much-is-too-much

Hoh, J. M., & Dhanashree, B. (2017). Antifungal effect of cow's urine distillate on Candida species. *Journal of Ayurveda and Integrative Medicine, 8*(4), 233–237. https://doi.org/10.1016/J.JAIM.2017.04.009

James L Madara. (2020, August 13). *American Medical Association Dietary Guidelines Letter.* American Medical Association. https://pcrm.widen.net/s/m2mwbvtbpg/2020-8-13-american-medical-association-dietary-guidelines-letter

Jarald, E. E., Edwin, S., Tiwari, V., Garg, R., & Toppo, E. (2008). Antidiabetic Activity of Cow Urine and a Herbal Preparation Prepared Using Cow Urine. *Pharmaceutical Biology*, *46*(10–11), 789–792. https://doi.org/10.1080/13880200802315816

Johnsen, J. F., de Passille, A. M., Mejdell, C. M., Bøe, K. E., Grøndahl, A. M., Beaver, A., Rushen, J., & Weary, D. M. (2015). The effect of nursing on the cow-calf bond. *Applied Animal Behaviour Science*, *163*, 50–57. https://doi.org/10.1016/j.applanim.2014.12.003

Jones, K. E., Patel, N. G., Levy, M. A., Storeygard, A., Balk, D., Gittleman, J. L., & Daszak, P. (2008). Global trends in emerging infectious diseases. *Nature*, *451*(7181), 990–993. https://doi.org/10.1038/nature06536

Kaur, G., Brar, Y., & Kothari, D. P. (2017). Potential of Livestock Generated Biomass: Untapped Energy Source in India. *Energies*, *10*(7), 847. https://doi.org/10.3390/en10070847

Khambadkone, S. G., Cordner, Z. A., Dickerson, F., Severance, E. G., Prandovszky, E., Pletnikov, M., Xiao, J., Li, Y., Boersma, G. J., Talbot, C. C., Campbell, W. W., Wright, C. S., Siple, C. E., Moran, T. H., Tamashiro, K. L., & Yolken, R. H. (2020). Nitrated meat products are associated with mania in humans and altered behavior and brain gene expression in rats. *Molecular Psychiatry*, *25*(3), 560–571. https://doi.org/10.1038/s41380-018-0105-6

Kmietowicz, Z. (2017). Red meat consumption is linked to higher risk of death from most major causes. In *BMJ (Online)* (Vol. 357). BMJ Publishing Group. https://doi.org/10.1136/bmj.j2241

Kole, R. K., Banerjee, H., & Bhattacharyya, A. (2001). Monitoring of market fish samples for endosulfan and hexachlorocyclohexane residues in and around Calcutta. *Bulletin of Environmental Contamination and Toxicology*, 67(4), 554–559. https://doi.org/10.1007/s001280159

Kristofer Hamel, Baldwin Tong, & Martin Hofer. (2019). Poverty in Africa is now falling—but not fast enough. In *Brookings*. https://www.brookings.edu/blog/future-development/2019/03/28/poverty-in-africa-is-now-falling-but-not-fast-enough/

Kumar, V., Majumdar, C., & Roy, P. (2008). Effects of endocrine disrupting chemicals from leather industry effluents on male reproductive system. *Journal of Steroid Biochemistry and Molecular Biology*, 111(3–5), 208–216. https://doi.org/10.1016/j.jsbmb.2008.06.005

Kumari, S., Hiloidhari, M., Kumari, N., Naik, S. N., & Dahiya, R. P. (2018). Climate change impact of livestock CH_4 emission in India: Global temperature change potential (GTP) and surface temperature response. *Ecotoxicology and Environmental Safety*, 147, 516–522. https://doi.org/10.1016/j.ecoenv.2017.09.003

Larry C. Price, & Debbie M. Price. (2017). India: Toxic Tanneries | Pulitzer Center. In *Pulitzer Center*. https://pulitzercenter.org/stories/india-toxic-tanneries

Lauren Frias. (2019, August 23). *Amazon losing about 3 football fields' worth of rainforest per minute*. Insider. https://www.businessinsider.com/amazon-losing-3-football-fields-worth-of-rainforest-per-minute-2019-8?op=1

Leather Industry: Indian Leather Exports & Manufacturers in India | IBEF. (2021). https://www.ibef.org/exports/leather-industry-india.aspx

Mahabharat (Hindi). (n.d.). GITA PRESS GORAKHPUR A UNIT OF GOBIND BHAWAN KARYALAYA, KOLKATA.

Meatpacking – Hazards and Solutions | Occupational Safety and Health Administration. (n.d.). Retrieved March 20, 2021, from https://www.osha.gov/meatpacking/hazards-solutions

Mekonnen, M. M., & Hoekstra, A. Y. (2012). A Global Assessment of the Water Footprint of Farm Animal Products. *Ecosystems*, *15*(3), 401–415. https://doi.org/10.1007/s10021-011-9517-8

Mikoczy, Z., & Hagmar, L. (2005). Cancer incidence in the Swedish leather tanning industry: Updated findings 1958-99. *Occupational and Environmental Medicine*, *62*(7), 461–464. https://doi.org/10.1136/oem.2004.017038

Min, K. B., & Min, J. Y. (2017). Association between leukocyte telomere length and serum carotenoid in US adults. *European Journal of Nutrition*, 56(3), 1045–1052. https://doi.org/10.1007/s00394-016-1152-x

Mónica Padilla de la Torre, Elodie F. Briefer, Brad M. Ochocki, Alan G. McElligott, & Tom Reader. (2016). *Mother--Offspring Recognition via Contact Calls in Cattle, Bos taurus.* https://www.wellbeingintlstudiesrepository.org/cgi/viewcontent.cgi?article=1126&context=acwp_asie

Ojedokun, A. T., & Bello, O. S. (2016). Sequestering heavy metals from wastewater using cow dung. In *Water Resources and Industry* (Vol. 13, pp. 7–13). Elsevier B.V. https://doi.org/10.1016/j.wri.2016.02.002

Oliver Laughland, & Amanda Holpuch. (2020, May 2). "We're modern slaves": How meat plant workers became the new frontline in Covid-19 war | Coronavirus | The Guardian. *Guardian.* https://www.theguardian.com/world/2020/may/02/meat-plant-workers-us-coronavirus-war

Ollie Davidson. (2020, November). *Millions of Minks Culled Due to COVID-19 Risk | Animal Equality | International Animal Protection Organization.* AnimalEquality. https://animalequality.org/blog/2020/11/24/millions-of-minks-culled-due-to-covid-19-risk/

Open Data Platform. (2021). Global Footprint Network. https://data.footprintnetwork.org/#/

Ornish, D., Lin, J., Chan, J. M., Epel, E., Kemp, C., Weidner, G., Marlin, R., Frenda, S. J., Magbanua, M. J. M., Daubenmier, J., Estay, I., Hills, N. K., Chainani-Wu, N., Carroll, P. R., & Blackburn, E. H. (2013). Effect of comprehensive lifestyle changes on telomerase activity and telomere length in men with biopsy-proven low-risk prostate cancer: 5-year follow-up of a descriptive pilot study. *The Lancet Oncology, 14*(11), 1112–1120. https://doi.org/10.1016/S1470-2045(13)70366-8

Ornish, D., Lin, J., Daubenmier, J., Weidner, G., Epel, E., Kemp, C., Magbanua, M. J. M., Marlin, R., Yglecias, L., Carroll, P. R., & Blackburn, E. H. (2008). Increased telomerase activity and comprehensive lifestyle changes: a pilot study. *The Lancet Oncology*, *9*(11), 1048–1057. https://doi.org/10.1016/S1470-2045(08)70234-1

Osman, K. M., Kappell, A. D., Orabi, A., Al-Maary, K. S., Mubarak, A. S., Dawoud, T. M., Hemeg, H. A., Moussa, I. M. I., Hessain, A. M., Yousef, H. M. Y., & Hristova, K. R. (2018). Poultry and beef meat as potential seedbeds for antimicrobial resistant enterotoxigenic Bacillus species: a materializing epidemiological and potential severe health hazard. *Scientific Reports*, *8*(1), 1–15. https://doi.org/10.1038/s41598-018-29932-3

Pan, W. R., Chen, P. W., Chen, Y. L. S., Hsu, H. C., Lin, C. C., & Chen, W. J. (2013). Bovine lactoferricin B induces apoptosis of human gastric cancer cell line AGS by inhibition of autophagy at a late stage. *Journal of Dairy Science*, *96*(12), 7511–7520. https://doi.org/10.3168/jds.2013-7285

Park, S., Kim, S. K., Kim, J. Y., Lee, K., Choi, J. R., Chang, S. J., Chung, C. H., Park, K. S., Oh, S. S., & Koh, S. B. (2019). Exposure to pesticides and the prevalence of diabetes in a rural population in Korea. *NeuroToxicology*, *70*, 12–18. https://doi.org/10.1016/j.neuro.2018.10.007

PETE MCBRIDE. (2014, August 6). *Industry on the Banks: Deep Inside Kanpur's Tanneries*. National Geographic. https://www.nationalgeographic.com/photography/article/industry-on-the-banks-deep-inside-kanpurs-tanneries

Pimentel, D., Acquay, H., Biltonen, M., Rice, P., Silva, M., Nelson, J., Lipner, V., Giordano, S., Horowitz, A., & D'Amore, M. (1992). Environmental and Economic Costs of Pesticide Use. *BioScience*, *42*(10), 750–760. https://doi.org/10.2307/1311994

Pimentel, D., & Pimentel, M. (2003). Sustainability of meat-based and plant-based diets and the environment. *American Journal of Clinical Nutrition*, *78*(3 SUPPL.). https://doi.org/10.1093/ajcn/78.3.660s

Pinheiro Machado, T. M., Machado Filho, L. C. P., Daros, R. R., Pinheiro Machado, G. T. B., & Hötzel, M. J. (2020). Licking and agonistic interactions in grazing dairy cows as indicators of preferential companies. *Applied Animal Behaviour Science*, *227*, 104994. https://doi.org/10.1016/j.applanim.2020.104994

Poverty in Africa: Facts & figures - SOS Children's Villages USA. (n.d.). Retrieved March 19, 2021, from https://www.sos-usa.org/about-us/where-we-work/africa/poverty-in-africa

Power of Positivity. (2020, March 17). *Study Finds that Cows Talk and Show Compassion Just Like Humans.* https://www.powerofpositivity.com/cows-talk-show-compassion/

R, P. K. T., Nishanth, B. C., S, P. K., Kamal, D., Sandeep, M., & Megharaj, H. K. (2010). Available online through Cow Urine Concentrate: A potent agent with Antimicrobial and Anthelmintic activity. *Journal of Pharmacy Research*, *3*(5), 1025–1027.

Randhawa, G. K., & Sharma, R. (2015). Chemotherapeutic potential of cow urine: A review. *Journal of Intercultural Ethnopharmacology*, *4*(2), 180–186. https://doi.org/10.5455/jice.2015022210032

Ranganathan, J., Vennard, D., Waite, R., Dumas, P., Lipinski, B., & Searchinger, T. (2016). *Shifting Diets for a Sustainable Food Future.* http://www.worldresourcesreport.org.

Rani, L., Thapa, K., Kanojia, N., Sharma, N., Singh, S., Grewal, A. S., Srivastav, A. L., & Kaushal, J. (2021). An extensive review on the consequences of chemical pesticides on human health and environment. In *Journal of Cleaner Production* (Vol. 283, p. 124657). Elsevier Ltd. https://doi.org/10.1016/j.jclepro.2020.124657

Raut, A. A., & Vaidya, A. D. B. (2018). Panchgavya and cow products: A trail for the holy grail. In *Journal of Ayurveda and Integrative Medicine* (Vol. 9, Issue 1, pp. 64–66). Elsevier B.V. https://doi.org/10.1016/j.jaim.2017.12.005

Richter, B. D., Bartak, D., Caldwell, P., Davis, K. F., Debaere, P., Hoekstra, A. Y., Li, T., Marston, L., McManamay, R., Mekonnen, M. M., Ruddell, B. L., Rushforth, R. R., & Troy, T. J. (2020). Water scarcity and fish imperilment driven by beef production. *Nature Sustainability*, *3*(4), 319–328. https://doi.org/10.1038/s41893-020-0483-z

Rob Cook. (2021, March 17). *World Beef Consumption: Ranking Of Countries - Beef Market Central*. Beef Market Central. https://beefmarketcentral.com/story-world-beef-consumption-ranking-countries-146-106879

SARAH GIBBENS. (2019, August 22). Brazil's Amazon is burning in historic wildfires—and deforestation is to blame. *National Geographic*. https://www.nationalgeographic.com/environment/article/wildfires-in-amazon-caused-by-deforestation

Sarah Holder. (2019, August 23). *The Burning of the Amazon, in 7 Maps and Graphs - Bloomberg*. Bloomberg CityLab. https://www.bloomberg.com/news/articles/2019-08-22/the-burning-of-the-amazon-in-7-maps-and-graphs

Sathasivam, A., Muthuselvam, M., & Rajendran, R. (2010). Antimicrobial activities of cow urine distillate against some clinical pathogens. *Global Journal of Pharmacology*.

Schneider, M. (2014). Developing the meat grab. *Journal of Peasant Studies*, *41*(4), 613–633. https://doi.org/10.1080/03066150.2014.918959

Shahin, M. (2018). The effects of positive human contact by tactile stimulation on dairy cows with different personalities. *Applied Animal Behaviour Science*, *204*, 23–28. https://doi.org/10.1016/j.applanim.2018.04.004

Shams, K. M., Tichy, G., Sager, M., Peer, T., Bashar, A., & Jozic, M. (2009). Soil contamination from tannery wastes with emphasis on the fate and distribution of tri- and hexavalent chromium. *Water, Air, and Soil Pollution*, *199*(1–4), 123–137. https://doi.org/10.1007/s11270-008-9865-y

Soil and Land Resources Assessment Division. (2016). *Indian Land Degradation Data Set*. https://bhuvan-app3.nrsc.gov.in/data/download/tools/document/land_degradation.pdf

Thin Lei Win. (2020). *Are working conditions in the meat industry fostering pandemics?* https://news.trust.org/item/20200612121508-ftbpr/

Troy Farah. (2020, July 2). US rivers and lakes are shrinking for a surprising reason: cows | Colorado | The Guardian. *Guardian*. https://www.theguardian.com/environment/2020/jul/02/agriculture-cattle-us-water-shortages-colorado-river

Tsachidou, B., Hissler, C., Noo, A., Lemaigre, S., Daigneux, B., Gennen, J., Pacaud, S., George, I. F., & Delfosse, P. (2021). Biogas residues in the battle for terrestrial carbon sequestration: A comparative decomposition study in the grassland soils of the Greater Region. *Journal of Environmental Management, 286*, 112272. https://doi.org/10.1016/j.jenvman.2021.112272

Tyagi, S., Siddarth, M., Mishra, B. K., Banerjee, B. D., Urfi, A. J., & Madhu, S. V. (2021). High levels of organochlorine pesticides in drinking water as a risk factor for type 2 diabetes: A study in north India. *Environmental Pollution, 271*, 116287. https://doi.org/10.1016/j.envpol.2020.116287

U.S. could feed 800 million people with grain that livestock eat, Cornell ecologist advises animal scientists | Cornell Chronicle. (1997, August 7). Cornell Chronicle. https://news.cornell.edu/stories/1997/08/us-could-feed-800-million-people-grain-livestock-eat

Uwizeye, A., de Boer, I. J. M., Opio, C. I., Schulte, R. P. O., Falcucci, A., Tempio, G., Teillard, F., Casu, F., Rulli, M., Galloway, J. N., Leip, A., Erisman, J. W., Robinson, T. P., Steinfeld, H., & Gerber, P. J. (2020). Nitrogen emissions along global livestock supply chains. *Nature Food, 1*(7), 437–446. https://doi.org/10.1038/s43016-020-0113-y

van de Kamp, M. E., van Dooren, C., Hollander, A., Geurts, M., Brink, E. J., van Rossum, C., Biesbroek, S., de Valk, E., Toxopeus, I. B., & Temme, E. H. M. (2018). Healthy diets with reduced environmental impact? – The greenhouse gas emissions of various diets adhering to the Dutch food based dietary guidelines. *Food Research International*, *104*, 14–24. https://doi.org/10.1016/j.foodres.2017.06.006

Vets pull out 71 kg of waste from stray cow's stomach. (2021, March 4). *Business Today.* https://www.businesstoday.in/latest/trends/vets-pull-out-71-kg-of-waste-from-stray-cows-stomach/story/433013.html

Vishwa Mohan. (2018, December 22). Sea levels could rise by up to 2.8 feet in India, says govt | India News - Times of India. *The Times of India.* https://timesofindia.indiatimes.com/india/sea-levels-could-rise-by-up-to-2-8-feet-in-india-says-govt/articleshow/67201466.cms

Weis, T. (2013). The meat of the global food crisis. *Journal of Peasant Studies*, *40*(1), 65–85. https://doi.org/10.1080/03066150.2012.752357

Westhoek, H., Lesschen, J. P., Rood, T., Wagner, S., de Marco, A., Murphy-Bokern, D., Leip, A., van Grinsven, H., Sutton, M. A., & Oenema, O. (2014). Food choices, health and environment: Effects of cutting Europe's meat and dairy intake. *Global Environmental Change*, *26*(1), 196–205. https://doi.org/10.1016/j.gloenvcha.2014.02.004

When consumers go vegan, how much meat will be left on the table for agribusiness? - Kearney. (n.d.). Kearney. Retrieved March 19, 2021, from https://www.kearney.com/consumer-retail/article?/a/when-consumers-go-vegan-how-much-meat-will-be-left-on-the-table-for-agribusiness-

WHO. (2015, October 26). *Cancer: Carcinogenicity of the consumption of red meat and processed meat*. World Health Organization. https://www.who.int/news-room/q-a-detail/cancer-carcinogenicity-of-the-consumption-of-red-meat-and-processed-meat

Willett, W., Rockström, J., Loken, B., Springmann, M., Lang, T., Vermeulen, S., Garnett, T., Tilman, D., DeClerck, F., Wood, A., Jonell, M., Clark, M., Gordon, L. J., Fanzo, J., Hawkes, C., Zurayk, R., Rivera, J. A., de Vries, W., Majele Sibanda, L., … Murray, C. J. L. (2019). Food in the Anthropocene: the EAT–Lancet Commission on healthy diets from sustainable food systems. In *The Lancet* (Vol. 393, Issue 10170, pp. 447–492). Lancet Publishing Group. https://doi.org/10.1016/S0140-6736(18)31788-4

Zhong, V. W., van Horn, L., Greenland, P., Carnethon, M. R., Ning, H., Wilkins, J. T., Lloyd-Jones, D. M., & Allen, N. B. (2020). Associations of Processed Meat, Unprocessed Red Meat, Poultry, or Fish Intake with Incident Cardiovascular Disease and All-Cause Mortality. *JAMA Internal Medicine*, *180*(4), 503–512. https://doi.org/10.1001/jamainternmed.2019.6969